From Your Friends at **The MAILBOX®**

Quick & Easy
SCIENCE FUN

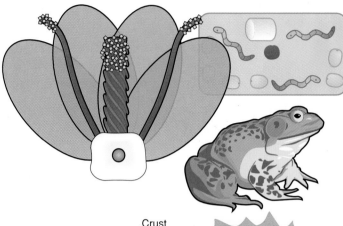

Crust

Mantle

Core

Sun's Layers

Core
Radiative Zone
Convection Zone
Photosphere
Chromosphere
Corona

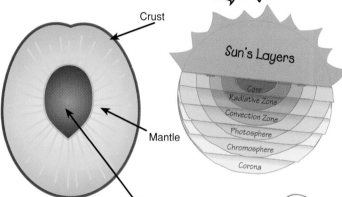

Table of Contents

Earth Science

Physical Science

About This Book

Designed to add zest to your science curriculum, *Quick & Easy Science Fun* is a wonderful collection of over 100 simple science experiments, activities, and demonstrations. Students will explore the wonders of science, develop science skills, and learn about a wealth of earth, life, and physical science topics through fun individual, small-group, and whole-class activities. These activities are perfect for supplementing your existing science curriculum. The pick-and-choose nature of the book allows you to quickly find just the right experiment, activity, or demonstration to complement your science curriculum. Although easy to implement and fun, *Quick & Easy Science Fun* activities provide students with meaningful science experiences that support the National Science Education Standards.

Quick & Easy Science Fun

Managing Editors: Deborah T. Kalwat, Jennifer Munnerlyn
Editor at Large: Diane Badden
Contributing Editor: Christa New
Writers: Tina Cassidy, Diane Coffman, Mary Jo Fessenmaier, Beth Gress, Beth Havill, Kimberly Minafo, Kathleen Scavone, Patricia Twohey, Janice P. Wittstrom, Cynthia Wurmnest
Copy Editors: Sylvan Allen, Karen Brewer Grossman, Karen L. Huffman, Amy Kirtley-Hill, Debbie Shoffner
Cover Artist: Clevell Harris
Art Coordinator: Rebecca Saunders
Artists: Nick Greenwood, Ivy L. Koonce, Sheila Krill, Clint Moore, Greg D. Rieves, Rebecca Saunders, Stuart Smith, Donna K. Teal
Typesetters: Lynette Dickerson, Mark Rainey

President, The Mailbox Book Company™: Joseph C. Bucci
Director of Book Planning and Development: Chris Poindexter
Book Development Managers: Elizabeth H. Lindsay, Thad McLaurin, Susan Walker
Curriculum Director: Karen P. Shelton
Traffic Manager: Lisa K. Pitts
Librarian: Dorothy C. McKinney
Editorial and Freelance Management: Karen A. Brudnak
Editorial Training: Irving P. Crump
Editorial Assistants: Hope Rodgers, Jan E. Witcher

Biomes and Ecosystems

Ecosystem Balance

Use this simple visual demonstration to help students understand the delicate balance of an ecosystem. In advance, copy, enlarge, and cut apart the plant and animal pictures below. Draw a picture of the sun on the board. Arrange the pictures on the board in order from producers to consumers to decomposers. Next, explain to students that each member of the ecosystem has an important job. After pointing out each organism's job, remove one of the pictures. Ask students what they think will happen if that organism is taken from the ecosystem. *(If a consumer is removed, there may be an overpopulation of producers. If a producer is removed, a consumer may die out due to a lack of food. If a decomposer is removed, the soil will lose nutrients and producers may not grow easily.)* If desired, extend this activity by discussing how other elements—such as pollution, human population, and introduction of new consumers—can affect an ecosystem.

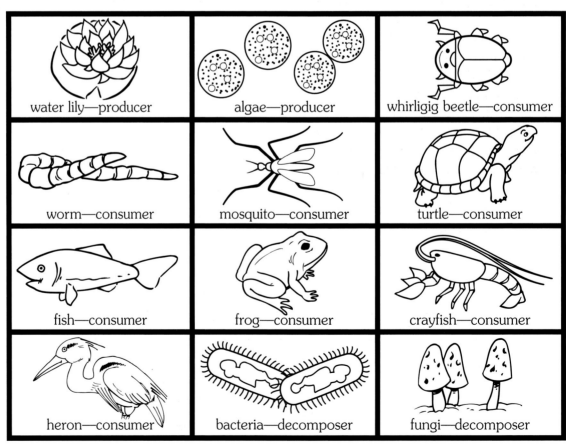

water lily—producer	algae—producer	whirligig beetle—consumer
worm—consumer	mosquito—consumer	turtle—consumer
fish—consumer	frog—consumer	crayfish—consumer
heron—consumer	bacteria—decomposer	fungi—decomposer

Web Weavers

Catch students' interest with this easy food web activity. In advance, cut two six-foot lengths of yarn for each student. Also, write "sun" and the name of each plant or animal from the list on a different index card. Next, give each student a card and two lengths of yarn. Instruct each student to read her card and then find a classmate whose card is connected to hers in the food web. Have the student hold one end of the yarn and give the connected classmate the other end. Direct each student to find as many connections as she can. Have extra lengths of yarn handy for students to make additional connections. When all the connections have been made, students will be surprised to see that the entire class is joined in one big web!

fox	ground beetle	meadow plants	person	bear
mole	robin	fungi	garter snake	ant
earthworm	caterpillar	cow	toad	bat
rabbit	falcon	bee	deer	box turtle
squirrel	grasshopper	fly	raccoon	seeds and nuts
snail	mouse	spider	owl	fruits and berries

Adaptation Anim-o

Reviewing animal adaptations is simple with this bingo game! First, write the names of animals you have discussed in class or animals from the list below each on a separate index card. On the board, write different types of animal adaptations, such as specialized mouth parts, specialized body parts, protective covering, camouflage, chemical defense, and mimicry. Next, give each student a sheet of white paper and bingo chips. Have each student make a bingo board by dividing the paper into a five-by-five grid and then randomly filling in the boxes with the different adaptations listed above. To play, call out the name of an animal from the set of cards. Instruct each student to cover a space on his board for that animal's adaptation. Remind students to place just one chip per animal even though some animals may have more than one adaptation. Continue playing until one student covers five words in a row (across, down, or diagonally) and calls out, "Anim-o!"

Specialized Mouth Parts	Specialized Body Parts	Protective Covering
baleen whale woodpecker hawk mosquito octopus	flying squirrel turtle puffer fish duck elephant	turtle armadillo porcupine rhinoceros crocodile
Camouflage	Chemical Defense	Mimicry
chameleon katydid Arctic fox flounder deer	skunk poison-arrow frog scorpion cobra bumblebee octopus	viceroy butterfly king snake stick insect tiger swallowtail butterfly caterpillar hoverfly

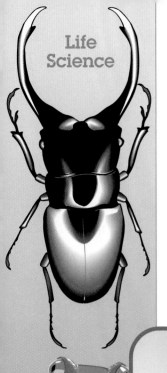

My Home in the Biome

Review biomes with this easy class game. First, program a class set of index cards each with a different plant or animal from the various biomes studied. Write each biome on the board. To play, ask a student volunteer to stand in front of the board. Have the volunteer close her eyes while you draw a card and show it to the class. Direct students to take turns giving the volunteer clues about the animal or plant's biome. For example, if the card is for an Arctic fox, a student might say the biome is extremely cold and that lichen or low shrubs grow there. When the volunteer has guessed the correct biome, have her tape the card to the board in that biome's column. Repeat this process with a new volunteer.

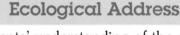

Ecological Address

Assess students' understanding of the different biomes with this quick group activity. Ahead of time, mask the biome names and make one copy of the clue cards shown below. Cut them apart and mount each card on a separate three-inch tagboard square. Next, divide students into six groups and give each group a clue card without revealing which biome the card represents. Direct each group to read its card and determine the biome the clues describe. Finally, have each group read its clues aloud and explain to the class which biome they represent.

Deciduous Forest	Tropical Rain Forest	Desert
cold winters; warm, wet summers broadleaf trees deer, raccoons, small birds Many animals have small bodies so they can move through the underbrush easily.	heavy rainfall, warm broadleaf evergreen trees, climbing vines colorful birds, monkeys, snakes Tree frogs have long toes with sticky tips to help them climb wet trees.	extremely dry sparse grasses, small-leaved shrubs small rodents, lizards, snakes Plants store water in thick leaves. Reptiles have tough, scaly skin that prevents water loss.
Taiga	Tundra	Grassland
cold winters, short growing season evergreen trees bears, moose, ducks A waxy covering protects tree needles from the cold and limits water loss.	extremely cold, dry low shrubs, lichens Arctic foxes, polar bears, migratory birds Arctic foxes and other animals grow thick white coats to blend into the snowy landscape.	temperate grasses antelope, bison, elephants Roots grow just below the surface of the soil and spread out to take in as much rain as possible.

Cells

Review "Cello-bration"

Watch your students wiggle with delight when they review the structures of plant and animal cells with these easy models. In advance, gather the materials listed below. Line the baking dish with plastic wrap. Then, 1½ hours before beginning the activity, make both the green and red Jell-O by following the directions on the box. Pour all of the green Jell-O into the baking dish. Fill each plastic bag with a half cup of the red Jell-O. Seal the bags and stand them in a large bowl. Then place the bowl and the baking dish in the refrigerator. When the Jell-O has thickened, complete the activity by following the directions below. Then serve the chilled cells to each pair. Before eating, encourage students to compare the two cells.

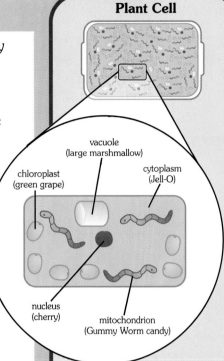

Plant Cell

vacuole (large marshmallow)

chloroplast (green grape)

cytoplasm (Jell-O)

nucleus (cherry)

mitochondrion (Gummy Worm candy)

Materials:

FOR PLANT CELLS
two 6 oz. boxes of green Jell-O
9" x 12" baking dish
plastic wrap
bag of large marshmallows
green grapes

FOR ANIMAL CELLS
several 6 oz. boxes of red Jell-O (1 box makes 5 bags)
½ cup measuring cup
quart-size freezer bags for half of your class
large bowl
bag of small marshmallows

FOR BOTH CELLS
large jar of whole cherries
large bag of Gummy Worm candies

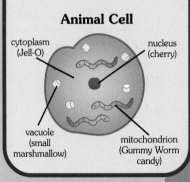

Animal Cell

cytoplasm (Jell-O)

nucleus (cherry)

vacuole (small marshmallow)

mitochondrion (Gummy Worm candy)

Directions:
1. Place the green Jell-O, large marshmallows, grapes, and approximately half of the cherries and Gummy Worm candies on a desk or table. Place the bags of red Jell-O and the remaining food items at a different location.
2. Ask students to recall the plant and animal cell organelles. List responses on the board.
3. Explain to students that they will make models of plant and animal cells using Jell-O and other food items. Have them choose from the provided food items to represent each organelle. List each representation beside the corresponding organelle on the chalkboard.
4. Divide students into pairs. Have half of the pairs each make an animal cell model by placing the food items into a bag of Jell-O, and sealing the bag. Have each of the remaining pairs make a plant cell model by placing the food items into a small section of the green Jell-O.
5. Repeat Step 4, allowing pairs to make the other type of cell.
6. After each pair has made both cells, cover the baking dish with plastic wrap and place the plastic bags back in the bowl. Return the Jell-O cells to the refrigerator for four hours.

Plants

Seed Savvy

Your students will be budding botanists after completing this easy plant comparison activity. In advance, gather several samples of seed-bearing plants and spore-bearing plants. Place each sample on a different paper plate labeled with the plant's name. Display the plant samples around the room. Next, review with students the difference between the two types of plants. Instruct each student to divide a sheet of notebook paper in half and label one column "Seed-Bearing Plant Samples" and the other "Spore-Bearing Plant Samples." Then direct the student to observe each plant sample and write its name in the appropriate column. When every student has categorized the plants, follow up with a class discussion to compare results.

Seed-Bearing Plant Samples	Spore-Bearing Plant Samples
apple	fern
pea (in pod)	moss
rose	seaweed
pinecone	mushroom
walnut	

Food on the Move

Show students how plants absorb food with this quick demonstration. In advance, gather the materials listed below for each pair of students. On the day of the activity, mix green food coloring with a gallon of water. Then pour a half cup of the colored water into a paper cup for each pair. Explain to students that most plants need a continuous supply of water, so water is absorbed through a process called *osmosis*. Then have student pairs observe osmosis in action by providing each pair with the materials listed and guiding them through the directions shown below.

Materials:
FOR EACH PAIR
half of a paper towel
paper cup
$^1/_2$ cup of green
    water
tape
scissors

Directions:
1. Starting at one of the short ends, roll the paper towel to make a tight stem. Tape the center with three parallel pieces of tape.
2. Slide one scissor blade in the center of one end of the roll. Make four long cuts. Then spread out the pieces to represent the root system.
3. Slide the scissor blade underneath the outer towel layer at the top of the stem. Make a cut; then fold the paper towel down to form a petal as shown. Continue cutting and folding petals until a small roll, representing the pistil, remains in the center of the paper towel flower.
4. Fan the root ends and place them in the water.
5. Observe as the green coloring moves up the roots and stem and into the petals.

Flower Power

Here's a fast and fun way to assess your students' knowledge of plant parts. Review with students the parts of a plant. Next, give a 4" x 6" index card and a straw to each student. Instruct the student to draw and color a flowering plant on the blank side of her index card. Have her label each part and write its function as shown. Then direct each student to write her name on the lined side of the card and tape the straw to the back. If desired, edge a strip of Styrofoam with green construction paper. Place each student's plant drawing in the Styrofoam and display in a windowsill or on a shelf. Label the display "Our Class Has Flower Power."

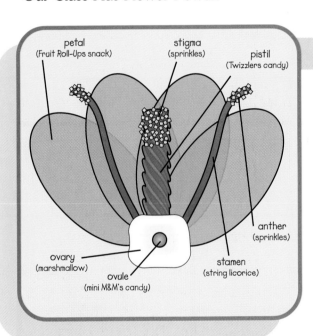

"Plant-astic" Treats

Students will really dig into this tasty review of flower reproduction. Ahead of time, gather the materials listed for each student. To begin the activity, ask students to recall the reproductive parts of a flower. List student responses on the board. Next, divide students into groups of four. Distribute the materials listed to each student. Then guide students through the directions below to make a cross-sectional model of a flower. As a class, discuss the reproductive functions of each plant part. Finally, invite students to consume their blooms!

Materials:
FOR EACH STUDENT
piece of red string licorice
mini M&M's candy
½ of a large marshmallow
Fruit Roll-Ups snack

½ Twizzlers candy
sheet of waxed paper
scissors

FOR EACH GROUP
small cup of yellow
   decorative sprinkles
small cup of water

Directions for each student:
1. Use scissors to cut four or five petal shapes from the Fruit Roll-Ups snack. Arrange them on the waxed paper in a flower shape.
2. Dip one end of the Twizzlers piece in the water and then in the decorative sprinkles. Lay the piece in the middle of the petals to represent the pistil and stigma.
3. Place a mini M&M's candy in the marshmallow half as shown. Position the marshmallow at the base of the Twizzlers piece to represent the ovary and the ovule.
4. Cut a piece of red string licorice into two pieces. Dip one end of each piece in the water and then in the decorative sprinkles. Place one piece on each side of the pistil to represent the stamen and anther.

Go Dig

Help students review plant reproduction with this fun twist on a favorite card game. Duplicate and enlarge 11 copies of the plant reproduction card set shown. Make one copy of the game directions. Laminate the cards and directions. Cut apart the cards. Put the directions and cards in a resealable plastic bag and place the bag in a center. In turn, direct student pairs to visit the center to play the game.

Directions:

FOR TWO PLAYERS

1. Players shuffle the deck of cards and deal seven cards to each player.
2. Each player looks at his hand and lays down any complete plant reproduction card sets.
3. Player 1 asks Player 2 for a particular card in the set. If Player 2 has the card, he must give it to Player 1. If Player 2 does not have the requested card, he says, "Go Dig," and Player 1 draws from the deck.
4. If Player 1 is able to make a complete set, he lays the cards down. After he lays down his set, his turn ends.
5. Player 2 takes a turn in the same manner.
6. Play continues until one player has matched his entire hand and is out of cards. That player is declared the winner.

Pollination
Pollen lands on the stigma of the pistil.

Fertilization
A pollen tube grows down into the ovary. The male sex cell from the pollen grain joins with the female sex cell in the ovary.

Fruit
The ovary enlarges and begins to form a fruit.

Seeds
The ovary continues to enlarge and seeds that contain tiny plants begin to form.

New Life
The fruit ripens and releases the seeds.

Life Cycles

Riddle Me This

Review life cycles with this quick creative-writing activity. First, divide students into groups of three. Direct each group to choose a plant or an animal. Make sure that each group chooses a different organism. Next, have each group write a riddle about the organism and its life cycle without mentioning the organism's name. Finally, have a volunteer from each group read its riddle aloud to the class. Ask the class to solve the riddle.

Butterfly
My babies look nothing like me.
They crawl and graze on greens.
Soon they'll hang motionless,
Tucked inside a green shell
To emerge a beautiful creature,
And then identical we'll be!

Does this organism's life cycle begin with an egg?

Yes.

Name That Organism

Answer students' questions about life cycles with this fun review game. First, write on the board a list of plants and animals. Then divide students into pairs. To begin play, a player secretly selects a plant or an animal from the list on the board. The opposing player asks a yes-or-no question about the organism and its life cycle. The first player answers the question. The opposing player may ask another question or make a guess about the organism's identity. Play continues in this manner until the organism's identity is determined. If 20 or fewer questions have been asked or guesses have been made, the asking player receives one point. Then players switch roles and a new organism is chosen. The player with more points in the given time frame is declared the winner.

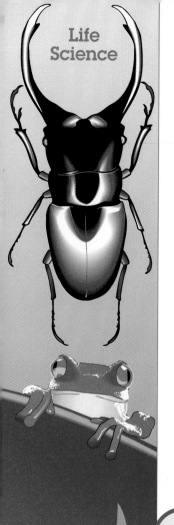

Examining Cycles

Get your students thinking critically with this quick activity. Write on the board the following list: tree, flower, insect, mammal, bird, reptile, fish, amphibian. Next, divide students into pairs and give each pair a sheet of white paper. Direct each pair to draw a Venn diagram on its paper. Then have the pair choose two organisms, each from a different category listed on the board. Instruct the pair to compare and contrast the organisms' life cycles. Remind students that similarities between the two organisms should be written in the overlapping section of the Venn diagram. When each pair is finished, have it share its diagram with the class.

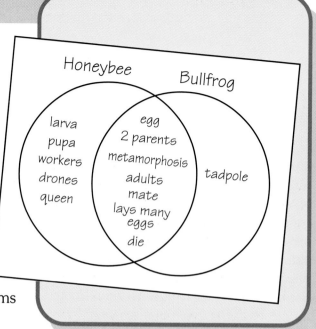

Station Identification

Use this simple station activity to assess students' understanding of life cycles. First, make a label for each station by writing on a different sentence strip each of the following life cycle stages: egg, larva, pupa, baby/infant, child, adolescent, seed, seedling, sapling, and adult. Place a supply of crayons and a different label in each station. Next, give each student a 4" x 6" index card.

Assign each student a different plant or animal and have him write it at the top of his card. Then direct each student to go to the station that represents the first stage of his organism's life. At that station, have the student draw and label a picture on his card to represent that stage. For example, if a student is assigned a fish, he goes to the egg station and draws a picture of a fish egg. Then ring a bell to signal students to move to the next stage. Repeat this process until each student has completed his life cycle card. Check each student's card for accuracy.

Vertebrates and Invertebrates

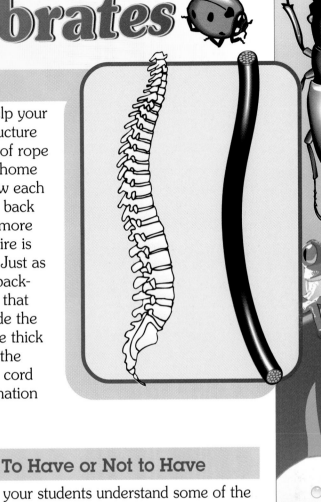

Hardwired

Here's a quick demonstration that will help your students understand the importance and structure of the spine. Ahead of time obtain a length of rope and a piece of conduit wire from your local home supply store. Allow students to compare how each item feels. Then ask each child to touch the back of his neck and decide whether his spine is more like the rope or the wire. Explain that the wire is similar to the spine found in all vertebrates. Just as the wire is covered in plastic, the spine, or back-bone, has a series of bones called vertebrae that surrounds and protects the spinal cord. Inside the plastic covering are small wires similar to the thick bundle of nerves in the spinal cord. Finally, the wire can relay information just as the spinal cord contains pathways that carry sensory information to the brain.

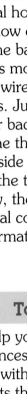

Vertebrates	Invertebrates
human	starfish
turtle	shrimp
snake	lobster
frog	ant
rabbit	crab
horse	bee
mouse	snail
dog	spider
fish	beetle
bear	jellyfish
eagle	sponge
lizard	worm

To Have or Not to Have

Help your students understand some of the differences between vertebrates and invertebrates with this classifying activity. Explain to students that *vertebrates* are animals that have backbones and *invertebrates* are animals without backbones. Further explain that vertebrates have *internal skeletons* (skeletons inside the body) made of bone or cartilage. Inform students that vertebrates include mammals, amphibians, birds, fish, and reptiles. Tell students that many invertebrates have *exoskeletons* (skeletons outside the body). Inform students that invertebrates include insects, worms, crabs, lobsters, sponges, snails, and jellyfish. Next, have each student make two columns on a sheet of notebook paper: one titled "Vertebrates" and the other "Invertebrates." Then read aloud the list above or write it on the board. Direct the student to write each word in the appropriate column. Ask student volunteers to share their answers with the class and explain how they classified each animal. (*Vertebrates—horse, eagle, rabbit, snake, human, dog, mouse, turtle, fish, frog, lizard, bear; Invertebrates—worm, ant, crab, snail, jellyfish, bee, shrimp, starfish, sponge, beetle, spider, lobster*)

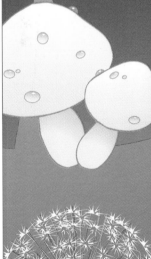

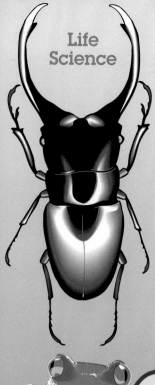

How Do Some Invertebrates Move?

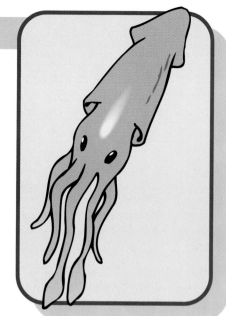

How can something move without a backbone? Use this "squid-sational" demonstration to help your students answer this question. Explain to students that a squid travels by jet propulsion, taking water in and pushing it out, which moves it *backward!* Demonstrate this unusual method of movement by squeezing the bulb end of a turkey baster. Put the tube end into a clear plastic tub of water and release the bulb so that it fills with water. Tell students that this action mimics a squid taking in water under its mantle. Next, squeeze the bulb again, forcing the water out of the tube. Explain that this mimics the action of a squid as it pushes water out through a funnel under its head, making it move backward.

Sponge Supper

As students soak up this super sponge activity, they will discover that some invertebrates, such as sponges, have a unique way of eating. Show students a natural sponge. Explain that it is really the sponge's skeleton that's been cleaned and dried. A live sponge has holes, or pores, through which water is squeezed to filter food. Let each student use a hand lens to examine the pores in a synthetic sponge. Then divide students into groups and guide them through the following experiment.

Materials:
FOR EACH GROUP
1 c. water
clear empty glass
1 tbsp. glitter
large-holed synthetic sponge (large enough to cover the top of the glass)
plastic spoon

Directions:
1. Use the spoon to stir the glitter (food) into the cup of water.
2. Place the sponge over the empty glass.
3. Predict what you think will happen to the food when it is poured on the sponge. Write your prediction.
4. Slowly pour the food (glitter mixture) onto the sponge.
5. Carefully fold the ends of the sponge together; then squeeze the sponge so that the water from it goes into the empty glass.
6. Record what happens to the food. *(The sponge filters the glitter from the water, trapping most of it in the sponge.)*

Quick Kingdom Roll

Roll out a quick review of the classification of living organisms with this easy game. Divide students into groups of three. Provide each group with an enlarged copy of the cube pattern shown and access to scissors and tape. Direct the group to cut out the pattern, fold along the solid lines, and then tape the tabs to form a cube. On the top of a sheet of notebook paper, have the group write the kingdoms shown on the cube. To play the game, have each group follow the steps below.

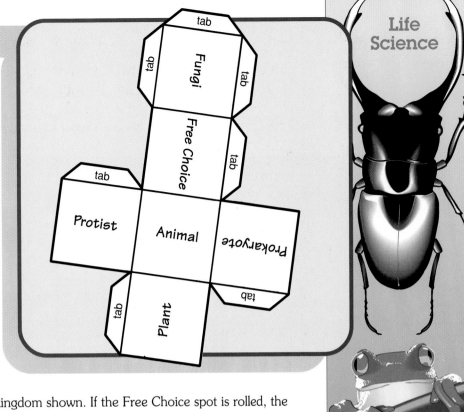

Directions:
1. Player 1 rolls the cube and reads the kingdom shown. If the Free Choice spot is rolled, the player chooses a kingdom.
2. Player 1 writes his initials and the name of a living organism from that kingdom in the correct column on the paper. If his partners disagree with the organism he listed, Player 1 erases his answer.
3. Each player takes a turn in the same manner.
4. After a set amount of time, the player who listed the most organisms is declared the winner.

Look-Alikes

Look-Alikes

- worm/snake
- caterpillar/centipede
- moth/butterfly
- bird/bat
- lobster/crab
- grasshopper/cricket
- turtle/snail

Do you think you're seeing double? Use this quick comparison activity to help your students see beyond how an animal looks and learn the differences between some easily mistaken identities. To begin, program a transparency with the names of animal pairs. Display the transparency. Have each student fold a sheet of notebook paper in half lengthwise. Direct him to choose one of the animal pairs from the overhead. Have the child write each animal name at the top of one side of his paper. Challenge the student to compare the animals by writing about their differences (for example, the animal's body type, how it moves, how it reproduces, or how it adapts in a dangerous situation). After three to five minutes, invite students to gather in small groups to share how they compared the same set of animals.

Life
Science

The Skeletal System

Body Builders

Use a little X-ray vision to introduce students to the skeletal system. In advance, enlarge the skeleton shown. Cut out each bone (or group of bones) and place a small Velcro piece on the back. Position a small connecting Velcro piece on a bulletin board for each bone. Next, explain to students that there are about 206 bones in the adult human body and each bone has a specific job. Give a bone to each student. Have the student place the bone in the correct position on the bulletin board. Ask the student to hypothesize what job the bone performs for the body (movement, protection, or framework). Use the bulletin board as a reference throughout your study of the skeletal system.

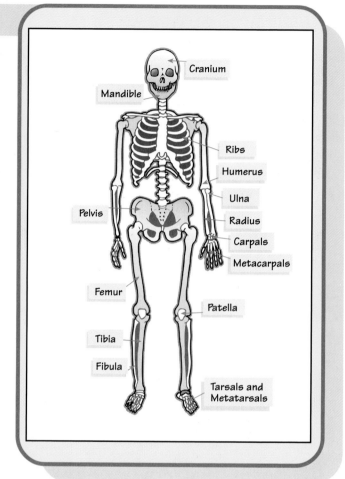

"Bone-anza"

Make no bones about it! Your students will love this skeletal system review game. Enlarge the skeleton shown above and copy the game directions below. Write the name of each bone on a different index card. Then cut out the skeleton, omitting the bone labels. Place the skeleton, cards, and game directions in a center. Provide scrap paper for students to keep score. Direct pairs of students to take turns playing the game.

Directions:
1. Shuffle the cards and lay the deck facedown. Lay the skeleton on the playing surface.
2. Player 1 draws a card and locates the indicated bone on the skeleton. Player 1 lays the card beside the bone and receives one point for correctly identifying the bone. If Player 1 indicates the wrong bone, she does not receive a point and loses her turn.
3. Player 2 may receive a bonus point for placing the card correctly.
4. Player 2 takes a turn in the same manner.
5. Play continues until each the card has been placed in the correct position on the skeleton. The player with more points is declared the winner.

©The Education Center, Inc. • *Quick & Easy Science Fun* • TEC1754

Out of Joint

Show students how difficult movement would be without joints with this simple activity. Explain to students that because bones are hard and rigid, movement without joints would be difficult. Further explain that joints are the places where bones meet. Ask students to try different movements without bending their arms, legs, fingers, or torso. For example, ask each student to tie his shoe without bending or to pick up a pencil and write his name while keeping his fingers straight. Students will quickly see that everyday activities are impossible without joints!

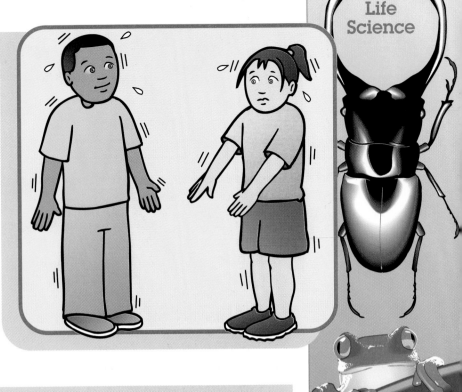

That's One Classy Joint!

Help students bone up on the different types of joints with this easy observation activity. Make a transparency of the chart shown and project it onto the board. Next, have each student list on a sheet of paper all the points on the body where there is movement between bones *(shoulder, elbow, wrist, thumb, fingers, neck, hips, knees, ankles, toes)*. Ask each student to isolate and carefully study the movement at each joint. Then instruct the student to compare that movement to the motion listed on the board. Direct the student to classify each joint on his paper. Finally, have student volunteers demonstrate the movement at each joint and discuss with the class what type of joint they think it is *(shoulder—ball and socket, elbow—hinge, wrist—gliding, thumb—saddle, fingers—hinge, neck—swivel, hips—ball and socket, knees—hinge, ankle—gliding, toes—hinge)*.

Type of Joint	Example of Motion
Hinge	Door
Immovable	No motion
Ball and socket	Ball on the bottom of a computer mouse
Saddle	Base of a joystick
Swivel	Twist-off jar lid
Gliding	Swing

©The Education Center, Inc. • *Quick & Easy Science Fun* • TEC1754

The Skeletal System **17**

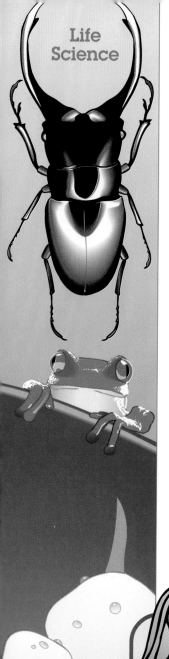

The Muscular System

Sort It Out

Introduce your students to the two types of muscles with this simple sorting activity. First, write the muscles from the chart in random order on the board. Next, have each student fold a sheet of notebook paper in half vertically and label the resulting columns Group 1 and Group 2. Direct the student to study the list of muscles on the board and then sort them by writing each muscle in a column on his paper. When students are finished, ask them to share their lists and explain how they categorized the muscles. Explain to students that the body contains voluntary and involuntary muscles. *Voluntary* muscles are muscles that move when you consciously decide to contract or relax them. *Involuntary* muscles contract because they are triggered by the nervous system. Finally, check the list on the board and discuss which muscles are voluntary and which ones are involuntary. Point out that even when the body is at rest, muscles are always working.

Voluntary Muscles
arm muscles
hand muscles
leg muscles
neck muscles
foot muscles
head muscles

Involuntary Muscles
stomach muscles
cardiac muscle
large intestine muscles
esophagus muscles
artery muscles

You "Knee-d" Muscles!

Show students how muscles and bones team up with each other with this small-group activity. Remind students that the kneecap is a bone and explain that the bone's movement is controlled by muscles. Next, divide students into pairs and have each pair position two chairs facing each other. Direct each partner, one at a time, to raise one pant leg above her knee, sit in a chair, and place her feet in the opposite chair, keeping the toes pointed straight up. Tell each partner to tighten or contract the upper leg muscle and watch as the kneecap moves. Then have each pair find other bones of the body that move by contracting muscles. Invite each pair to share one muscle-and-bone movement with the class.

Multimuscle Movement

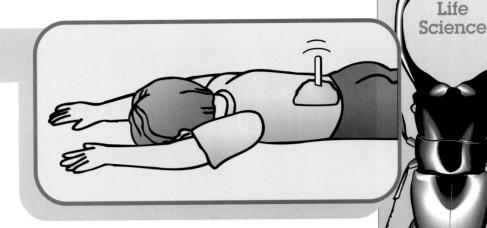

Bulk up students' understanding of the muscular system with this easy movement activity. Divide students into pairs and give each pair a small ball of clay and a wooden craft stick. Instruct the pair to shape the clay into a ball with a flat bottom and then insert the wooden craft stick in the top. Next, have one student in each pair lie on his stomach with his head flat and arms and legs outstretched as shown. Direct his partner to place the clay ball on the student's back toward the lower part of the spine. Instruct the student on the floor to move his arm up toward the ceiling. Have his partner watch the craft stick to see if it moves. Repeat this process with the other arm, the head, and then each leg. Then have partners switch places and repeat the activity. Students will easily see that their muscles move together as a system.

Work Those Muscles!

Here's a handy way to demonstrate that voluntary muscles require more energy than involuntary muscles. Ahead of time, gather a class supply of wooden spring-type clothespins and a stopwatch. Next, explain to students that the muscular system is responsible for all of the body's movements. Different muscles move different parts of the body, and some muscles require more energy than others. Ask students to hypothesize which type of muscle requires more energy—involuntary or voluntary. Then give each student a clothespin and instruct her to stand beside her desk. Have the student pinch her clothespin open with her non-dominant hand and try to hold it open for three minutes. If the student cannot hold the clothespin open, direct her to sit down when she closes it. Then instruct each student to sit and place two fingers on his pulse (either on his neck or wrist) for three minutes. At the end of three minutes, discuss with students which activity took more energy—holding open the clothespins or their hearts beating.

The Digestive System

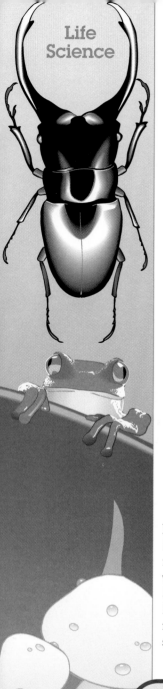

Break It Down!

Help your students understand how enzymes work in the digestive system with this simple demonstration. In advance, gather the materials listed below. Label one cup and paper plate "Plain" and a different cup and plate "Enzyme." Fill the third cup with water. Next, explain to students that the body produces special chemicals called enzymes to aid in digestion. Further explain that enzymes break food down into smaller pieces. Then follow the directions below to complete the demonstration. Discuss with students the differences in the two gelatin balls. Ask students what they think happened to the gelatin when the meat tenderizer was added. *(The meat tenderizer acted as an enzyme and caused the gelatin to stay soft.)*

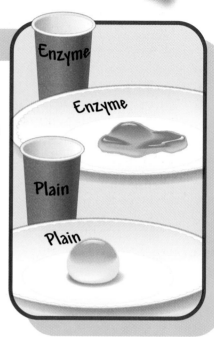

Materials:
2 packets unflavored gelatin
meat tenderizer
water
3 plastic cups
2 paper plates
measuring spoons
spoon

Directions:
1. Empty one gelatin packet into each of the labeled cups.
2. Stir two teaspoons of water into the "Plain" cup. As the gelatin becomes firm, mold it into a ball and place it on a paper plate.
3. Stir two teaspoons of water and one-fourth teaspoon of meat tenderizer into the "Enzyme" cup. When the gelatin thickens, place it on the other paper plate.
4. Pass the plates around for students to observe the gelatin mixtures.

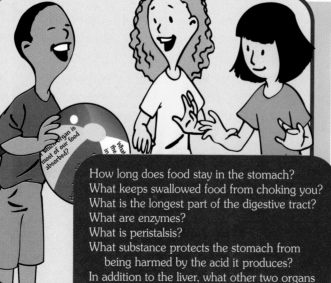

How long does food stay in the stomach?
What keeps swallowed food from choking you?
What is the longest part of the digestive tract?
What are enzymes?
What is peristalsis?
What substance protects the stomach from being harmed by the acid it produces?
In addition to the liver, what other two organs produce enzymes for the digestive system?

Having a Ball

Toss a little fun into your review of the digestive system with this game. Inflate a large beach ball. Use a permanent marker to write 15 to 20 questions (see the examples) about the digestive system on the ball. Next, toss the ball to a student. Have him read aloud and answer the question under his right thumb. Then direct the student to toss the ball to a classmate and repeat the process. Continue playing until each student has taken a turn.

The Story of Digestion

Use this easy creative-writing review to assess your students' understanding of the digestive system. First, ask students to recall the order of the digestive organs as you write them on the board *(mouth, esophagus, stomach, liver, pancreas, gallbladder, small intestine, large intestine)*. Next, give each student a 12" x 18" sheet of white construction paper. Direct each student to create six sections by folding the paper in half vertically, folding it into thirds, and then unfolding it. Have each student create a cartoon showing a food particle traveling through each of the digestive organs. Remind students that each frame of the cartoon should show what happens to the food as it is digested. If desired, display students' cartoons on a bulletin board titled "Food on the Move."

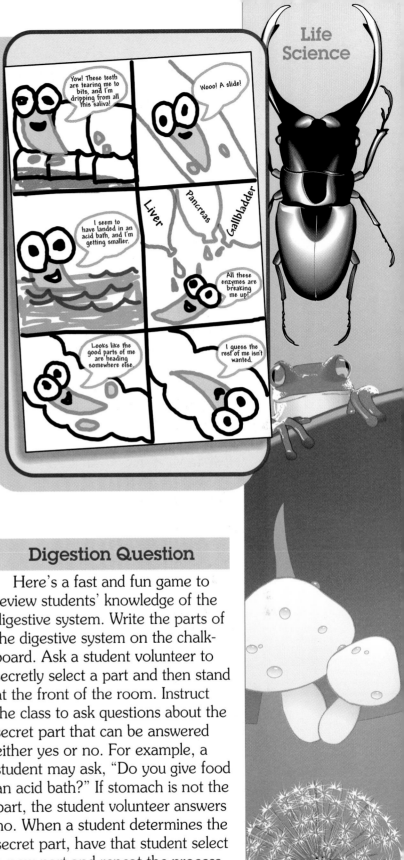

Digestion Question

Here's a fast and fun game to review students' knowledge of the digestive system. Write the parts of the digestive system on the chalkboard. Ask a student volunteer to secretly select a part and then stand at the front of the room. Instruct the class to ask questions about the secret part that can be answered either yes or no. For example, a student may ask, "Do you give food an acid bath?" If stomach is not the part, the student volunteer answers no. When a student determines the secret part, have that student select a new part and repeat the process.

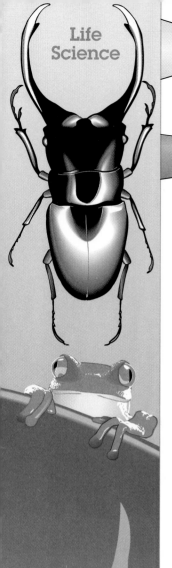

The Circulatory System

Poetry From the Heart

Introduce the circulatory system with this simple poetry activity. Write the following poem on a chart and post it on the board. Have students follow along as you read the poem aloud. Next, ask students to identify the different parts of the circulatory system mentioned in the poem as you underline them *(blood, heart, blood vessels)*. Then discuss each part's job based on the poem. *(Blood vessels transport blood throughout the body. The heart pumps blood. The blood carries oxygen.)*

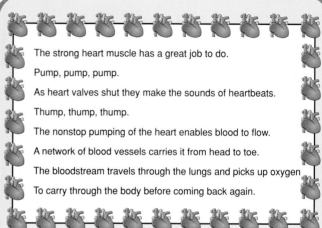

The strong heart muscle has a great job to do.

Pump, pump, pump.

As heart valves shut they make the sounds of heartbeats.

Thump, thump, thump.

The nonstop pumping of the heart enables blood to flow.

A network of blood vessels carries it from head to toe.

The bloodstream travels through the lungs and picks up oxygen

To carry through the body before coming back again.

The Beat Goes On and On and...

Use this quick demonstration to show students how hard the circulatory system works to keep the body supplied with blood. Ask four volunteers to stand at the front of the classroom. Tell the first student to act as the brain by continually tapping his head and saying, "Beat, heart. Beat, heart." Have the second student also be the brain by tapping on her head and saying, "Breathe, lungs. Breathe, lungs." Tell the third student to act as the lungs by raising her arms above her head each time she inhales and dropping them by her sides as she exhales. Have the fourth student be the heart by continually squeezing a tennis ball with his hand. Start the volunteers simultaneously and time them for three minutes. At the end of three minutes, stop the volunteers and discuss the difficulty of each job. Ask students if they would be able to perform all of the jobs at once. Remind students that the body automatically performs these jobs each day all day long.

Never Skips a Beat

Help students understand just how hard the heart works with this simple simulation. Ahead of time, gather two Styrofoam bowls, a timer, and a teaspoon for each group of three students. Fill one bowl with water for each group. To simulate the heart's job, divide students into groups of three and guide them through the directions below. Point out to the class that when the heart pumps blood through the body, it is similar to transferring water from one bowl to another. Ask students if they think they could continue the simulation for the rest of the day without getting tired. Students will quickly realize that the heart does an amazing job keeping the body supplied with blood.

Directions:
1. Each group member selects a job: timekeeper, counter, or worker.
2. The timekeeper announces the start of one minute and sets the timer.
3. The worker uses the teaspoon to transfer water from the full bowl to the empty bowl. The counter counts how many teaspoons of water are transferred.
4. The timekeeper announces the end of one minute and the worker stops.

heart
pumps
squeezes
muscle
chambers
moves
hardworking
valve
automatic
constant
blood
pulse
pounds
heartbeats

The Circulatory System

Circulation Charts

Review the parts of the circulatory system with this group activity. Divide students into small groups and give each group three large sheets of white paper. Instruct the group to write a different part of the circulatory system (blood, heart, blood vessels) at the top of each paper. Next, tell the students in each group to name as many words as they can to describe the heart and write them on the paper labeled "heart." Time the groups for one minute. Repeat this process for blood vessels and blood. Finally, collect all of the papers and hang them on the board, grouping the same parts together. Have volunteers read and discuss the descriptions on each poster.

The Respiratory System

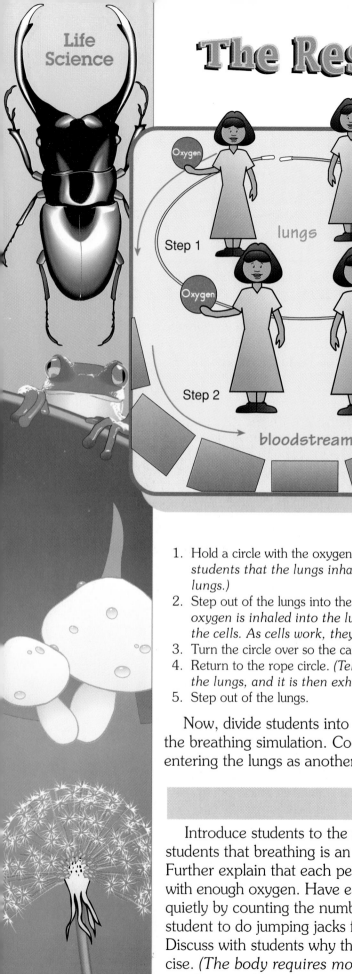

The Ins and Outs of Breathing

Develop students' understanding of breathing basics with this group simulation. Have each student cut out a large blue circle and label it "Carbon Dioxide." Tell the student to also cut out a same-sized red circle and label it "Oxygen." Direct each student to glue his circles back to back. Next, form a large circle on your classroom floor with a long jump rope. Move students' desks to create a circular path around the rope as shown. Then demonstrate for students the breathing process by following these steps:

1. Hold a circle with the oxygen side facing out. Walk to and enter the rope circle. *(Explain to students that the lungs inhale oxygen. Tell students that the rope circle represents the lungs.)*
2. Step out of the lungs into the circular pathway and begin walking around. *(Explain that when oxygen is inhaled into the lungs, it is absorbed into the body's bloodstream and carried to the cells. As cells work, they produce a waste product called carbon dioxide.)*
3. Turn the circle over so the carbon dioxide side shows.
4. Return to the rope circle. *(Tell students that the bloodstream carries carbon dioxide back to the lungs, and it is then exhaled out of the body.)*
5. Step out of the lungs.

Now, divide students into groups of three. In turn, direct each group to repeat the breathing simulation. Coordinate the timing of the groups so that one group is entering the lungs as another group is leaving.

Breathing Rate

Introduce students to the respiratory system with this easy activity. Explain to students that breathing is an essential process that the body does automatically. Further explain that each person breathes at different rates to keep his body supplied with enough oxygen. Have each student check his breathing rate while he is sitting quietly by counting the number of times he inhales in one minute. Next, direct each student to do jumping jacks for one minute and then check his breathing rate again. Discuss with students why their breathing rate is higher during and right after exercise. *(The body requires more oxygen and the way to get it is to breathe at a quicker rate.)*

Breath of Fresh Air

Use this easy demonstration to show students how the nose works as a screen for the respiratory system. Ahead of time, coat the opening and inside of a clear, narrow-necked bottle with honey. Next, explain to students that the bottle represents the nose and the honey represents the mucous membrane. Further explain that the mucous membrane is a sticky lining inside the nose and the entire respiratory tract. It helps keep small particles out of the lungs. Then hold the bottle at an angle and sprinkle a small amount of dark-colored glitter into the opening. Tell students that the glitter represents small particles in the air. Finally, show students that the honey traps the glitter just as the mucous membrane traps particles before they reach our lungs.

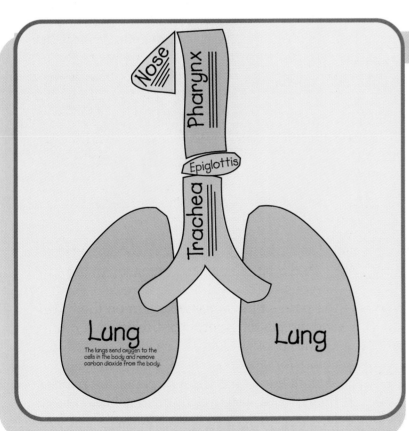

Nose
Pharynx
Epiglottis
Trachea
Lung

The lungs send oxygen to the cells in the body and remove carbon dioxide from the body.

Lung

Breathing Space

Breathe easy as students work through this quick review of the respiratory system. Write the parts of the respiratory system (*nose, pharynx, epiglottis, trachea, lungs*) on the board. Divide students into groups of five and give each group member a different-colored sheet of light-colored construction paper. Next, have each group member choose a different part of the respiratory system. Direct the student to draw and cut out his part. Then have him label the part and write its part's job on the cutout. When all members of a group are finished, instruct them to put the parts together to make a complete respiratory system. Ask each group member to explain his part as he puts it into position. As a variation, have each group race to correctly place the parts of the respiratory system.

The Nervous System

You're on My Nerves!

Introduce your students to the nervous system with this simple experiment. Divide students into pairs and give each pair two Q-tips and two toothpicks. Instruct Partner 1 to roll up her sleeve and turn her head away from Partner 2. Direct Partner 2 to lightly touch Partner 1's upper arm with the two Q-tips close together and then again with them further apart. Have Partner 1 write down what she feels. Next, direct Partner 2 to lightly touch Partner 1's lower arm and palm with the Q-tips in the same manner. Instruct Partner 1 to again write down what she feels with each touch. Have Partner 2 repeat all the touches with the toothpicks while Partner 1 records her feelings. Then direct the partners to switch roles and repeat the experiment. Ask students how they know when they are being touched. *(Nerves send signals to the brain.)* Finally, discuss the results of the experiment with your class.

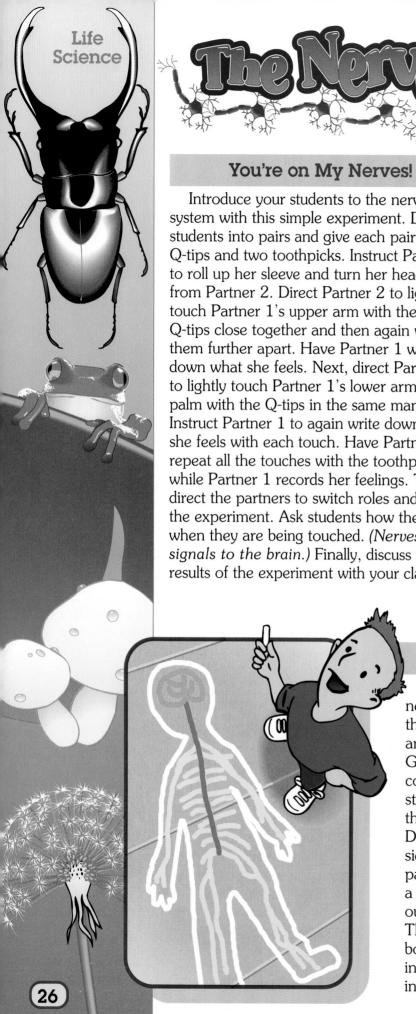

Sidewalk Sketch

Add a bit of color to your study of the nervous system with this easy review. First, list the parts of the nervous system on the board and write a different color beside each one. Gather enough sidewalk chalk in each of those colors for students to use. Next, have each student copy on a sheet of paper the parts of the nervous system and the matching colors. Divide students into pairs and take them outside to a sidewalk. (Have students take their papers with them.) Place the sidewalk chalk in a central location. Direct each pair to draw the outline of one partner's body on the sidewalk. Then instruct the pair to draw and color on the body each part of the nervous system according to the color key. Check each pair's drawing for accuracy.

Bundle of Nerves

Use this fun art activity to help students review how the nervous system operates. Remind students that the body's nervous system coordinates the activities of the body and helps it adjust to changes. Ask students to think of situations in which the body must respond quickly, such as burning a hand, catching a ball, moving out of the way of a swing, or slamming the brakes on a bike to avoid a crash. List students' suggestions on the board. Then give each student a sheet of white paper. Have each student choose a situation and draw the steps the body goes through to react to it. For example, a student could draw a hand being burned, the nerve carrying the signal to the muscle to trigger the reflex as well as to the brain, the muscles moving out of reflex, and the hand moving off the hot surface. Display students' pictures on a bulletin board titled "Nervous Reactions."

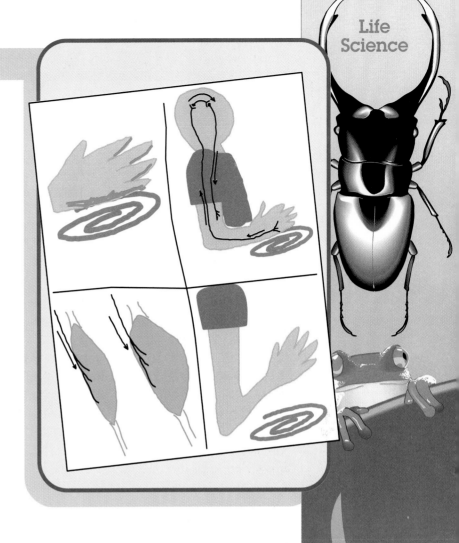

Dear Mr. New Body,

I am applying for the job of spinal cord. I am the best spinal cord for the job because I have never failed to carry a signal to the brain.

I've Got the Nerve!

Use this letter-writing activity to assess students' understanding of the nervous system. Write the parts of the nervous system on the board. Ask students to pretend that a new body is being made, and it is taking job applications for nervous system parts. Direct each student to choose a part to apply for and then write a letter to the body explaining why she should be chosen for the job. Remind each student to write from the point of view of the nervous system part and show that she understands its role. Finally, have each student share her letter with the class.

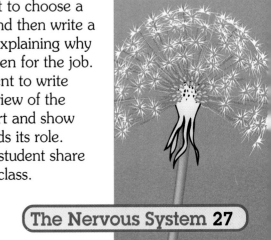

Structure of the Earth

Ocean Exploring

Fascinate your students with a simple experiment that helps explain why it is impossible for humans to explore the ocean floor at certain depths. Ahead of time gather one clean, empty milk carton for every three students (check with your school cafeteria). Then remind students that undersea vehicles with pressure-proof cabins are needed to study depths below 1,500 feet because of the intense pressure of the water. At this depth, the pressure would crush a person's lungs. Divide students into groups of three. Provide each group with the materials listed above and a copy of the directions shown below.

Materials:
FOR EACH GROUP
milk carton
scissors
large plastic bowl
masking tape
small bottle of water
permanent marker

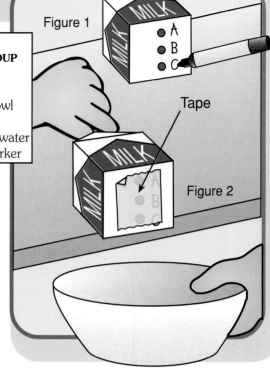

Figure 1

Tape

Figure 2

Directions:
1. Position the carton as shown; then use the scissors to carefully poke three holes of equal size and distance across the bottom of the milk carton. Label the holes "A," "B," and "C" (see Figure 1).
2. Cover the holes with tape.
3. Fill the carton with water.
4. Have the first group member tightly pinch the carton spout together. Then have her position the carton on a desk or tabletop with the taped side slightly over the edge.
5. Direct the second group member to hold the bowl under the carton to catch the water (see Figure 2).
6. Instruct the third group member to quickly pull off the tape and observe how the water flows from each hole. (*Because hole C is at a greater depth than the others, the water weight at that point causes a higher pressure. When the tape is removed, the water rushes out of hole C faster than the other two holes.*)

All out of the Ocean

Oil: Oil rigs drill for oil. It can be used in cars.

Sand and gravel: Gathered from the ocean floor. They can be used in concrete.

Fresh water: Created at desalinization plants. Could be used for drinking.

All out of the Ocean

Did you know that many items you come into contact with every day come from the ocean? Explain to students that besides providing food, the ocean provides us with many valuable resources, including minerals and energy. Challenge each child to research and list three items from the ocean, how they are obtained, and how the items might be used. Cover a bulletin board with dark blue paper. Then have each child use white chalk to write her list on the board. Title the board "All out of the Ocean."

A Look at Layers

This quick lesson will have your students visualizing the earth's layers and snacking on them too! Pair students. Give each pair a ripe plum, a plastic knife, and a small paper plate. Explain that the plum can be thought of as a model of the earth and its three main layers: the *crust,* the *mantle,* and the *core.* Direct the pair to carefully cut the plum in half. Point out that the tough outer skin of the plum represents the earth's crust, the fruit represents the mantle, and the pit can be thought of as the earth's core. If desired, choose student volunteers to relate facts about each layer. Finally, after the pairs are finished examining the model, allow each partner to enjoy his half of the plum.

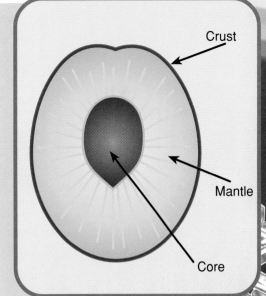

Mount St. Helens
(United States, 1980,
1 cubic km)

Vesuvius
(Italy, A.D. 79, 10 cubic km)

Mount Pinatubo
(Phillipines, 1991,
10 cubic km)

Mount Novarupta
(Alaska, 1912,
17 cubic km)

Krakatau
(Indonesia, 1883,
30 cubic km)

Tambora
(Indonesia, 1815,
95 cubic km)

Volcanoes!

Give students an opportunity to learn more about the awesome power of some past volcanic eruptions with this activity. To begin, explain to students that there are approximately 1,400 active volcanoes around the world today. Scientists study past eruptions to try to understand how and when future blasts might occur. Divide students into six groups. Assign each group a volcano from those shown at the left. Provide the group with construction paper, markers and crayons, and access to resource materials. Give each group a set amount of time to research when and where its volcano erupted and the size of the eruption based on the amount of pumice and ash released into the air. Next, have the group create a construction paper poster by recording the information about its volcano and drawing a picture of it erupting. Collect the posters. Then display them according to the size of each volcano's blast.

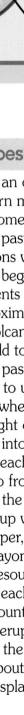

Forces on Earth

All About Our Atmosphere

This research-based bulletin board idea will have your students looking up as they study the layers of the earth's atmosphere. To begin, explain to students that the atmosphere is a moving mass of air stretching hundreds of miles above the earth. It protects the earth from the sun's rays and heat like a multilayered shield. Divide students into five teams. Direct each team to research one of the main layers of the atmosphere: *troposphere, stratosphere, mesosphere, thermosphere,* or *exosphere.* Allow the teams ten to 15 minutes to complete their research. Next, provide each team with a different-colored sheet of blue paper corresponding to the distance its atmospheric layer is from the earth (light blue paper for the layers closer to the earth and darker blue paper for layers that are farther away). Direct each team to cut its paper into an arc and then record information about its layer on the arc. Finally, collect the papers and display them one atop another on a bulletin board titled "All About Our Atmosphere."

All About Our Atmosphere

Exosphere

Thermosphere

Mesosphere

Stratosphere

Troposphere Troposphere is the lowest layer of the atmosphere. The height of this layer varies around the earth depending on the temperature of its air. At the warm equator the height is about 16 km. At the North and South Poles, the layer only reaches 9 km.

Pulled by Gravity

Items	Landed at the same time	Didn't land at the same time
pencil, penny	✓	
tissue, book		✓
marker, eraser	✓	
paper, pen		✓

Got Gravity?

Keep your students grounded with this quick small-group activity about gravity. To begin, remind students that gravity is the force that pulls objects toward the center of the earth. Point out that light objects and heavy objects fall at the same speed unless air resistance slows them down. Divide students into four groups. Then display a chart similar to the one shown. Give each group one of the pairs of items listed on the chart. To complete the gravity test, have one group member drop each object at the same time from the same height. Direct the other members of the group to observe the objects' fall. Record the outcome of each group's test on the chart. As a class, discuss each group's results. Finally, ask students why they think the tissue and the book did not reach the ground at the same time. *(Both items encountered air resistance, but the tissue acted more like a parachute, slowing its fall.)*

Great Gravity

Your students are sure to be dazzled by this demonstration on gravity. To begin, remind students that gravity helps keep the earth and the other planets in their orbits around the sun. Then gather the materials listed and complete the directions below. After the demonstration, ask students the following questions: Why did the cup remain on the tagboard swing? *(The cup stays on the swing because the swing is moving fast enough.)* How are the cup of water and the swing like the earth orbiting around the sun? *(Like the earth orbiting the sun, the water moves horizontally as it falls. At the top of the cup's orbit, water would fall from the cup if it were not moving. But it is moving, so by the time the water would have fallen, the cup has moved along its orbit to another spot that is at least as far below the top of the circle as the water would have fallen.)*

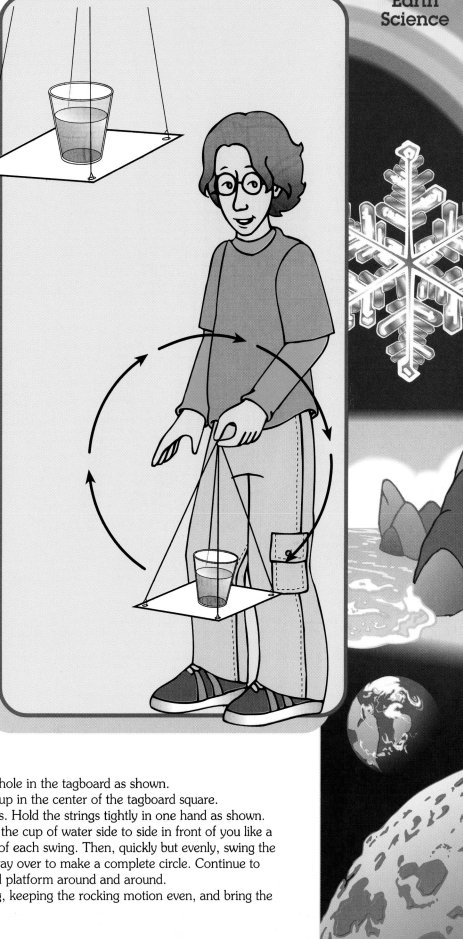

Materials:
3 oz. paper or plastic cup
5" x 5" tagboard square
four 3' lengths of string
hole puncher
water

Directions:
1. Punch a hole in each corner of the tagboard square.
2. Tie each length of string to a separate hole in the tagboard as shown.
3. Fill the cup ¾ full of water. Place the cup in the center of the tagboard square.
4. Gather all four strings by the loose ends. Hold the strings tightly in one hand as shown.
5. Gently rock the tagboard platform and the cup of water side to side in front of you like a swing. Gradually increase the distance of each swing. Then, quickly but evenly, swing the cup of water and the platform all the way over to make a complete circle. Continue to smoothly and evenly swing the cup and platform around and around.
6. To stop, gradually slow down the swing, keeping the rocking motion even, and bring the swing to a complete stop.

Sun and Moon

Flip for the Sun

Help students organize information about the sun's layers with this fun flip booklet. First, make a transparency of the directions and steps. Then explain to students that the sun is a huge ball of hot gases. In fact, the sun is large enough for the earth to fit inside it about one million times! Further explain that the sun has six layers, each with its own features and temperature. Next, distribute three sheets of white paper, scissors, and crayons to each child. Display the transparency and guide students through the directions to create a flip booklet illustrating each of the sun's layers. As students learn about the sun, instruct them to write the temperature and features of each layer on the appropriate flap in their flip booklets. If desired, have students add a decorated, construction paper semi-circle resembling the sun to the top of their booklets.

Directions:
1. Horizontally stack three sheets of paper so that the bottom edges are one inch apart. (Step 1)
2. Fold over the top half to form six layers. (Step 2)
3. Staple the booklet along the top edge. (Step 3)
4. Draw a large semicircle around the outside edge of the booklet. Then cut it out as shown. (Step 4)
5. Label the space on each flap with one of the sun's layers. (Step 5)
6. Starting from the folded edge, draw a semi-circle on each flap to represent each layer as shown. (Step 6)
7. Color the core red. Then color each of the remaining layers a different shade of red, orange, or yellow.
8. Write your name on the back of the booklet.

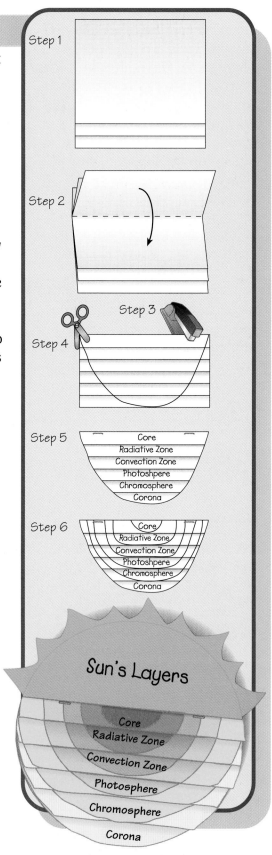

Step 1

Step 2

Step 3

Step 4

Step 5
Core
Radiative Zone
Convection Zone
Photoshpere
Chromosphere
Corona

Step 6
Core
Radiative Zone
Convection Zone
Photoshpere
Chromosphere
Corona

Sun's Layers
Core
Radiative Zone
Convection Zone
Photosphere
Chromosphere
Corona

The Sun Says...

Put a spin on your study of Earth's lunar and solar neighbors with this quick and easy game about the movements of the sun and moon. First, remind students that the earth, moon, and sun are in constant counterclockwise motion (see chart). Then review the difference between *rotation* (spinning on an axis) and *revolution* (revolving around another body). Next, tell students that they are going to play

The Sun Says, a game played similarly to Simon Says. To play, students walk counterclockwise around their desks when you announce, "The Sun says revolve." When you say, "The Sun says rotate," each student stands in place and turns in a counterclockwise circle. Demonstrate each type of movement. Direct each student to stand beside his desk. Alternately announce rotating and revolving movements with other motions as played in Simon Says. Continue play until one student remains standing. That player is declared the winner.

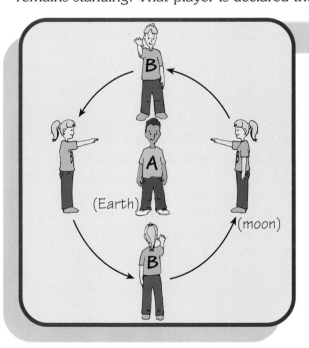

(Earth)

(moon)

Moon Motion

This easy movement activity is sure to help students understand why we only see one side of the moon. Explain to students that unlike the sun and the earth, the moon completes a revolution and rotation in the same amount of time. The moon revolves around the earth and rotates on its axis once every 27 1/3 days. For this reason, only the moon's near side can be viewed from Earth. To simulate this idea, divide students into pairs. Have each pair stand in an open area where movement won't be restricted. Then have one partner in each pair (Partner A) represent the earth and the other partner (Partner B) represent the moon. Have Partner B face Partner A with a raised arm as shown. Instruct Partner B to revolve around Partner A, keeping her back facing away from him as she moves. Direct Partner A to carefully observe Partner B's movement. Point out that when Partner B has made one complete revolution, she has also made one complete rotation. Have students change roles and repeat the demonstration.

PLANETS

Meaningful Memorization

Get students more involved in remembering the order of the planets with this creative twist on an old favorite. Write "My Very Educated Mother Just Served Us Nine Pizzas" on the chalkboard. Explain to students that the sentence was created to help people remember the order of the nine planets in our solar system. Point out to students that the first letter of each word stands for one of the planets. Challenge each student to use a dictionary to help him write his own sentence to memorize the order of the planets. Direct each child to consider choosing and ordering words which together have meaning to him. (Extra words might be necessary.) Once the child has written his sentence, allow him to read it aloud to the class and explain how the words will help him remember the order of the planets.

Mary Visits Europe Monthly Just So Uncle Ned (can) Paint.

Planet Diameter (km)

Planet	Diameter
Mercury	4,900
Venus	12,100
Earth	12,756
Mars	6,800
Jupiter	142,800
Saturn	120,660
Uranus	52,400
Neptune	49,500
Pluto	2,300

Sizable Differences

Use this easy demonstration to help students better understand the relative size of each planet. First, show students a Ping-Pong ball. Explain to students that for this activity, one Ping-Pong ball represents 2,300 kilometers. Point out to students that because the diameter of Pluto is 2,300 kilometers, the size of the planet could be represented by one Ping-Pong ball. Next, display a chart similar to the one shown. Pair students. Direct each pair to use a calculator to determine approximately how many Ping-Pong balls it would take to represent the diameter of each of the other planets (*Mercury = 2, Venus = 5, Earth = 6, Mars = 3, Jupiter = 62, Saturn = 52, Uranus = 23, Neptune = 22*). Have the pair record its answers on a sheet of lined paper.

Planet Posters

If it were possible, which planet would you most like to visit? Here's a fun, fast-paced activity that will allow your students to answer this question in a creative way. To begin, divide students into eight groups. Assign each group a planet (excluding Earth). Give the group a sheet of tagboard, markers or crayons, and access to resource materials. Explain to the class that each group is a travel agency in charge of promoting its assigned planet. Direct the group to use the materials provided to make a poster that includes information such as the planet's size, unique characteristics, hazards, and available resources. After a set amount of time, have each group display its poster where the other students can read it. If desired, set aside time for students to vote for the planet they would most like to visit.

Make Mine Mars!

No lines.
No cars.
No people.

- See frozen deserts, craters, dunes, volcanoes, and canyons—all in shades of red.
- Get blown away by the supersonic wind speeds!
- Feel safe! Even though this planet was named for the Roman god of war, there are no battles being fought here!

Book your space flight today!

*Bring your own O_2 and H_2O.

Neptune has more moons than which of the following planets?

What are Saturn's rings made of?

Which of the following terms best describes Jupiter?

A. terrestrial, or Earthlike, planet
B. giant planet
C. small planet
D. moon-free planet

Planetary Play

Reinforce key concepts with this fun whole-class game. First, provide each child with three index cards. Instruct her to make up three questions about three different planets. Then have the child write each question on an index card and list four answers, one of which is correct, for each question. Direct her to label the answers A, B, C, and D. Using her pencil, have the student circle the correct answer as shown. Collect the cards. Quickly read over the questions and scan the answers. Mark through any repetitive questions. Next, divide the students into two teams. Choose a card and read it aloud. Give the first person on Team 1 ten seconds to identify the correct answer. If she succeeds, award her team a point. If she doesn't answer correctly it becomes Team 2's turn. Play continues in the same manner until every student has taken a turn. The team with more points is declared the winner.

Stars, Asteroids, and Comets

Super Stars

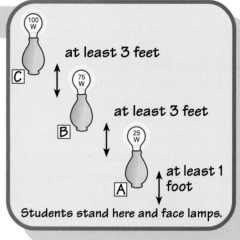

at least 3 feet

at least 3 feet

at least 1 foot

Students stand here and face lamps.

Use this simple demonstration to shine a little light on the difference between a star's *apparent magnitude* (how bright a star appears) and *absolute magnitude* (how bright a star actually is). Gather three table lamps, with the shades removed. Put each of the following lightbulbs in a lamp: 25 watt, 75 watt, and 100 watt. Identify the lamps as A, B, and C respectively, by taping a labeled index card to each lamp base. Determine where students will stand; then position the lamps in front of that spot as shown in the diagram. Turn off the overhead lights and have the students observe the brightness of the lamps. Call on a student volunteer to rate the lamps in order of their brightness. Then tell students the different wattages. Explain that the absolute magnitude of the lamps are the wattages of the bulbs. The apparent magnitude is how bright the light seems to be from where the students are standing. Similarly, a star like Sirius seems to be the brightest star because it is close to Earth. Other stars that look dim are actually brighter than Sirius, but their distance from Earth makes them seem fainter.

Fabulous Space Phenomenon

Stars, asteroids, and comets—oh my! This fun Venn diagram activity will allow your students to easily see the differences and similarities among these objects in space. Pair students. Provide each pair with an enlarged copy of the Venn diagram shown below, scissors, and access to a variety of resources on the solar system. After cutting out the pattern, encourage the partners to work together to research facts about stars, asteroids, and comets. Direct the pair to list information pertaining to each phenomenon in the correct space on the diagram. If a fact applies to more than one topic, have the students record the information in the area where the pictures overlap. If desired, create a larger copy of the Venn diagram to be displayed on a bulletin board and have each pair choose a fact to record. Set aside time for students to share what they have learned about these members of our solar system.

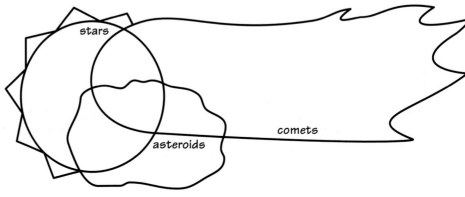

stars

asteroids

comets

Size Wise

Here's a fun way to help students compare the approximate sizes of stars within the five main star groups. Make an enlarged copy of the star patterns below for every child. Direct the student to cut out the patterns and arrange them in order from smallest to largest. Next, have students use reference materials to list the approximate size of the stars in each of the following groups: *neutron stars, white dwarfs, dwarf stars, giants,* or *supergiants.* Then have the student arrange the groups in order from smallest to largest. Have the student write the name of each star group on the corresponding pattern. Finally, have each student use a hole puncher to make a hole in the top of each pattern and then thread a length of string through the holes to make a small flip book.

Rocks and Minerals

Sandwich Squeeze

This sandwich isn't for eating; it's for showing how metamorphic rock is formed. Explain to students that one of the three types of rocks is *metamorphic* rock. Place several sheets of newspaper on the floor. Position a sheet of waxed paper on top of the newspaper. Stack three slices of bread on the waxed paper—a white slice between two dark slices. Cover the bread with another sheet of waxed paper. Walk across the "rock sandwich" several times. Next, cut the sandwich in half with scissors. Have each student describe the inside of the sandwich. Then explain to students that metamorphic rocks are formed by changes in *igneous* or *sedimentary* rocks (the slices of bread). Further explain that these rocks may be changed to metamorphic rocks by extreme heat and pressure (stepping on the bread). Inform students that metamorphic rocks are found beneath the earth's surface and are generally the hardest and densest of the three types of rock (bread after stepping on it). If desired, extend the demonstration by having each student define the three types of rocks—igneous, sedimentary, and metamorphic—in his science journal.

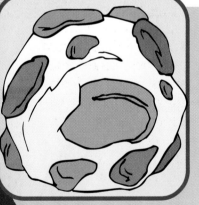

Create a Conglomeration!

This experiment won't put you on rocky ground, but it will teach students about how sedimentary rocks are formed. *Sedimentary* rocks are made over time from bits and pieces of rocks that have been deposited by wind, water, or glaciers. Divide students into groups of five. Then guide each group through the following directions to make a "quick" sedimentary rock. (For best results, allow to dry overnight.)

Materials:
paper cup
bowl (or the bottom of a plastic milk jug)
rocks and pebbles
$1/2$ c. plaster of paris
spoon
$1/4$ c. water
waxed paper

Directions:
1. Fill a cup with small rocks and pebbles.
2. In a bowl, combine plaster of paris and water. Stir it with a spoon until it is the consistency of pancake batter.
3. Shape the mixture into a ball and place it on waxed paper. Push the rocks and pebbles into the mixture.

Settlin' Down

It's settled. This activity is sure to help your students understand the concept of deposition. *Deposition* is the settling of materials carried by the agents of erosion—water, wind, and ice. Have students predict what will happen to rock particles of different sizes when they are deposited by water. Then divide students into groups of four to complete the following experiment. After students complete the experiment, ask the following questions: What happened to the jar's contents when the jar was set down? Do you see different layers on the bottom? What is different about the layers? How do you think materials settle in rivers and streams? If desired, have each student make a sketch of the jar, labeling each layer correctly.

Materials:
equal amounts of sand, gravel, and pebbles
large jar with lid
water

Directions:
1. Mix the sand, gravel, and pebbles in the jar.
2. Add water until the jar is about ³/₄ full.
3. Secure the lid on the jar.
4. Shake the jar carefully until the contents are thoroughly mixed.
5. Allow the contents to settle.
6. Observe how long it takes the materials to settle.

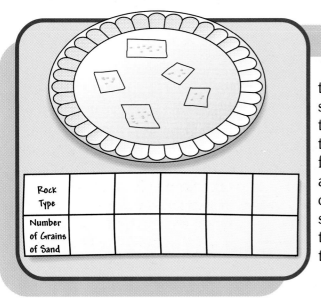

Rock Type					
Number of Grains of Sand					

Chip off the Old Rock!

Have you ever taken the time to look closely at several grains of sand? If you do, you might notice that each grain looks different from the next. That's because sand comes from rock particles. Have students act as investigators to explore the different rocks found in sand. Pair students. Provide each pair with the materials listed and a copy of the directions shown below.

Materials:
2 tbsp. sand in a small cup
hand lens
2 craft sticks
large white Styrofoam plate
access to reference books about rocks and minerals
paper and pencils

Directions:
1. Make a chart similar to the one shown.
2. Place three or four pinches of sand on the plate.
3. Look through the hand lens. Use the craft stick to separate the sand grains by color or other visible differences.
4. Draw a box around each sand group.
5. Use the reference books to determine the type of rock from which each sand group may have come.
6. Complete the chart by writing the rocks and the number of sand grains found for each type of rock.

Rock On...and On, and On!

This rousing review will have your students rehearsing the rock cycle over and over again! Begin by reminding students that the three main types of rocks—*sedimentary, metamorphic,* and *igneous*—are part of a never ending process called the *rock cycle.* Over time and under the right circumstances, each type of rock can evolve into either of the two other types. Because this cycle happens over and over again, the sedimentary rock you observe today might have been a metamorphic rock years ago, and could possibly be an igneous rock at some time in the future.

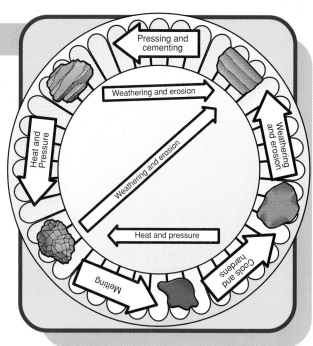

Provide each child with the materials listed and a copy of the patterns below. Then guide the student through the directions shown to make a rock-cycle review tool.

Materials:
large paper plate, scissors, glue, markers or crayons

Directions:
1. Cut out the rock-cycle patterns.
2. Think about the rock cycle and how different factors cause rocks to change into other types of rocks. Put the sedimentary rock pattern in the upper left-hand corner of the plate. Then place the other rock patterns and the short arrows around the edge of the paper plate. Place the long arrows in the middle of the plate.
3. Once the patterns correctly form the rock cycle, glue them onto the plate.
4. Complete the study tool by coloring the patterns.

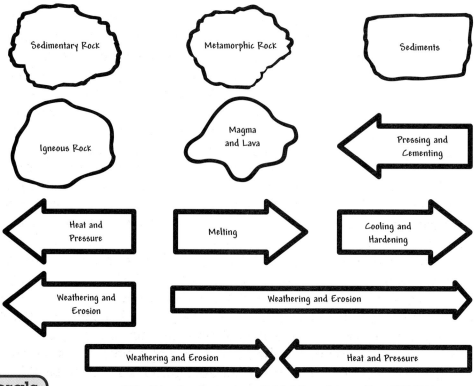

©The Education Center, Inc. • *Quick & Easy Science Fun* • TEC1754

Natural Resources: Conservation and Preservation

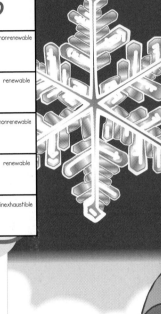

Resource-o!

Make learning about the different groups of natural resources easy with this variation of bingo. Make a class supply of bingo cards. Direct each student to use a pen to randomly label the top portion of each space on the card with one of the following terms: *renewable, nonrenewable,* or *inexhaustible.* Call out a natural resource. Direct each student to determine whether the resource is *renewable* (can be replaced), such as plants and animals; *nonrenewable* (cannot be replaced), such as coal, iron, and petroleum; or *inexhaustible* (cannot be used up), such as sunlight. Then have the child use a pencil to write the natural resource on a corresponding space on his bingo card as shown. Play continues in this manner until one student writes five natural resources in a row in any direction and calls out "Resource-o!" If he has written the words in the correct spaces, he is declared the winner. Direct players to erase the natural resources listed on their cards; then continue playing.

Resource-o

renewable	nonrenewable	inexhaustible sunlight	renewable	nonrenewable
inexhaustible	renewable	nonrenewable	inexhaustible	renewable
nonrenewable	inexhaustible	Free	renewable	nonrenewable
inexhaustible	renewable	nonrenewable	inexhaustible	renewable
nonrenewable	inexhaustible	renewable	nonrenewable	inexhaustible

water

Improper Use:

leaving the faucet running while you brush your teeth

Proper Use:

washing only full loads of laundry

Packed With Action

Get students out of their seats and on their feet with this lively activity on the proper and improper uses of natural resources. Divide students into groups of four. Provide each group with a blue, a red, and a black marker and four large index cards. Then post a list of natural resources where every group can see it. Have each group member choose a resource from the list. Direct the child to use the black marker to write the natural resource on the blank side of an index card. Then have him turn the card over and write the proper use of the resource on the right side of the card in blue and the improper use of the resource on the left side of the card in red. When each group is finished, have it place its cards in a paper lunch bag. Direct groups to swap bags. In turn, allow each group two minutes to choose a card from its bag and then act out either the proper or improper use of the natural resource listed on the card. Instruct the seated group members to guess the natural resource and the proper or improper use that is being depicted. After a group correctly guesses, award it a point. Then have the winning group take a turn acting out one of its natural resource cards. If a group's natural resource isn't correctly determined in the allotted amount of time, the group chooses another card and acts out that resource. After each group has enacted all of its cards, the group with the most points is declared the winner.

Changes in the Earth's Surface

Pangaea Puzzle

Introduce students to the theory of continental drift with this quick puzzle activity. To begin the activity, explain to students that scientists think the earth's continents were once a single, large land mass called *Pangaea*. Over time, the shifting of tectonic plates caused Pangaea to break apart. As a result, the continents slowly drifted toward their present positions. Next, provide each student with a copy of a world map, scissors, glue, crayons and a sheet of construction paper. Instruct the student to color and cut out the continents. Then have her reassemble the pieces to form a supercontinent. Direct the student to glue the supercontinent to her construction paper and then label it "Pangaea."

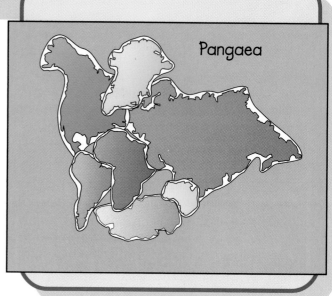

Pangaea

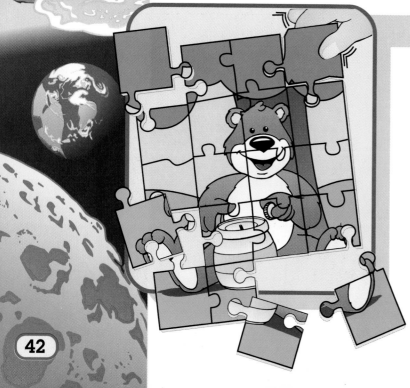

Reconstruction Dilemma

Use this easy puzzle activity to help students understand why an exact reconstruction of the supercontinent Pangaea is impossible. Divide students into groups of five. Distribute a small, well-used puzzle and several nail files to each group. Instruct the group to complete its puzzle. Then direct each group member to carefully remove a puzzle piece from the edge of the puzzle. Have the group member use a nail file to roughen up the edges of his puzzle piece. Then direct him to try to reposition it in the puzzle. Lead students to conclude that over time the shape of each continent has changed similarly to how the nail file changed the shape of the puzzle piece.

Mountains in the Making

Use these quick and easy demonstrations to peak students' interest in the different ways mountains are formed. In advance, gather two different-colored blocks of clay, a bottle of glue, a small piece of cardboard, an empty 20-ounce plastic drink bottle with lid, a balloon, and scissors. Then demonstrate for students how each type of mountain is formed by following the directions below.

Formation of a folded mountain:
(Appalachian Mountains, Himalayas, Alps, and Ural Mountains)
1. Explain to students that a folded mountain is formed when two tectonic plates collide and force rock upward.
2. Make two different-colored 1/2-inch-thick clay strips representing tectonic plates from the blocks of clay.
3. Place both tectonic plates on a flat surface. Push the plates together until a fold forms as shown.

Formation of a fault-block mountain:
(mountains in the Great Rift Valley, Grand Tetons, Sierra Nevada, and Wasatch Range)
1. Explain to students that a fault-block mountain is formed when masses of rock move up or down along a fault.
2. Make two different-colored 1/2-inch-thick clay strips representing tectonic plates from the blocks of clay.
3. Place both tectonic plates on a flat surface. Push one plate into the other so the first plate rises above the second as shown.

Formation of a dome mountain:
(Bighorn Mountains, Black Hills, Pikes Peak, and Sangre de Cristo Mountains)
1. Explain to students that a dome mountain is formed when the earth's surface is lifted up by magma, forming a bulge.
2. Cut off the bottom of the plastic bottle and the neck of the balloon. Stretch the balloon around the bottom of the bottle as shown.
3. Push the top of the balloon into the bottle. Point out to students that the balloon represents the surface of the earth and the air in the bottle represents magma.
4. Squeeze the bottle until the balloon rises.

Formation of a volcanic mountain:
(Mount Fuji, Mauna Loa, Mount Pinatubo, and Mount Saint Helens)
1. Explain to students that when magma erupts and continues to build up, it can form a volcanic mountain.
2. Cut a small hole in the piece of cardboard.
3. Open the cap of the glue bottle and slide the tip of the bottle through the cardboard hole.
4. Point out to students that the glue represents the magma and the cardboard represents the earth's surface. Squeeze the bottle until a small amount of glue flows on the cardboard.
5. Continue squeezing the glue, allowing it to build up on the cardboard.

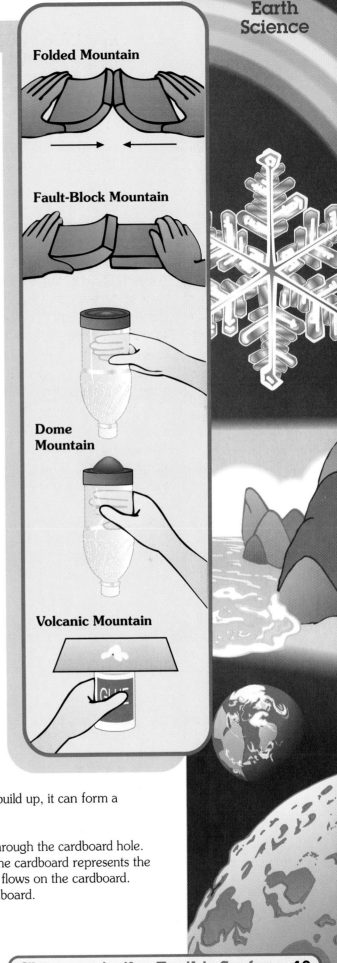

Folded Mountain

Fault-Block Mountain

Dome Mountain

Volcanic Mountain

Facing Weathering

Use this simple demonstration to show students that water can cause monumental problems. Ahead of time, fill a small balloon with water and place it in a bowl. Cover the balloon with Magic Shell chocolate sauce. Then place the bowl in the freezer overnight. Display a picture of Mount Rushmore. Explain to students that the memorial to four presidents is carved into a cliff in the Black Hills of South Dakota. Next, have students list problems the National Park Service might have maintaining the memorial. Then show students the frozen, candy-coated balloon. Have them observe the condition of the balloon's chocolate shell. Explain to students that as the water inside the balloon froze, it expanded, causing the shell to crack. Further explain that water causes weathering that can damage stone memorials. When water gets in the cracks in the rock and freezes, the cracks widen and the rock breaks into pieces.

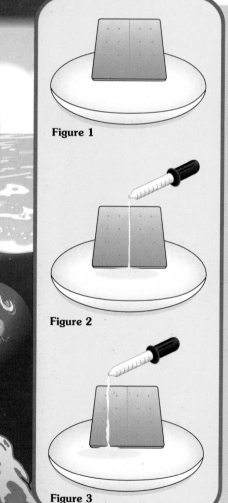

Figure 1

Figure 2

Figure 3

Weathering Effect

Develop students' understanding of one type of weathering with this fun activity. In advance, gather the materials listed for each pair of students. Then guide students through the directions below to demonstrate the effects of weathering by water. Finally, discuss the results of the demonstration. *(The movement of the water wears away parts of the cracker just as the movement of water wears away rock and soil.)*

Materials:
FOR EACH PAIR
2 graham cracker rectangles (connected)   plastic knife
deep-edged Styrofoam plate   eyedropper
1 tsp. frosting   small cup of water

Directions:
1. Use the knife to spread frosting on the edge of the paper plate. Then angle the cracker on top of the frosting with the perforation positioned vertically as shown. (Figure 1)
2. Fill the eyedropper with water. Hold the dropper above the perforation between the two crackers. Squeeze the water so that it runs down the perforation as shown. (Figure 2)
3. Observe the cracker and the water in the bottom of the plate.
4. Repeat this process over another area of the cracker. (Figure 3)
5. Continue dropping water on the cracker, alternating between the perforation and the other area of the cracker.
6. Observe the condition of the cracker and the water in the bottom of the plate.

Water

Make a Little Rain

Help your students review the water cycle with this easy demonstration. Ahead of time, fill an ice cube tray with water colored by food coloring; then freeze it to make colored ice cubes. Next, remove the labels from two empty, clean two-liter soda bottles. Then cut the tops off each bottle as shown. Position Bottle A on a desk or tabletop where every student can see it. Fill Bottle A half full of hot, but not boiling, water. Fill Bottle B with the ice cubes. Place Bottle B inside Bottle A so it rests just above the hot water as shown. Direct students to observe what happens inside Bottle A. Finally, have each student answer the questions below.

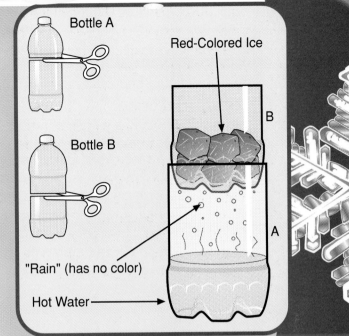

Bottle A

Bottle B

Red-Colored Ice

B

A

"Rain" (has no color)

Hot Water

Questions:
1. Which part of the model represented evaporation? *(the hot water)*
2. Which part of the model showed condensation? *(the water drops that formed on the bottom of the smaller bottle)*
3. Where was the "rain"? *(It was dripping into the hot water.)*
4. How do you know that the "rain wasn't just water leaking from Bottle B? *(The rain was not colored.)*

1. Oceans   S
2. Lakes   F
3. Rivers   F
4. Reservoirs   F
5. Wells   F
6. _____
7. _____
8. _____
9. _____
10. _____

Worldwide Water

Here's a quick activity that will drive home the importance of water conservation. Pair students. Challenge each pair to list ten different natural water sources (such as lakes, oceans, and rivers) on a sheet of lined paper. Next, have each pair write "F" next to the listed water sources that consist of freshwater and "S" next to the water sources that consist of salt water. Direct the partners to determine the percentage of freshwater sources in their list. Record the percentages on the board. Then show the students a clear jar full of water. Pour out 97 percent of the water, explaining that it represents the salt water in the world's oceans. Announce that the remaining 3 percent represents the world's freshwater. Pour out another 2 percent, explaining that this water is unavailable because it is frozen in ice caps and other glaciers. Tell students that half of the 1 percent remaining is groundwater (found beneath the earth's surface). Lastly, show students the remaining drops of water in the bottle. Explain that only about $^1/_{50}$ of 1 percent of the earth's water fills rivers and lakes.

Find the Finest Filter

Did you know we drink the same water the dinosaurs did? Use this fast and fun small-group activity to help students understand how filtration allows us to drink water that is millions of years old. To begin, explain to students that filtering is an important part of cleaning and treating water. Modern water treatment facilities use many different types of filters to trap unwanted particles and make the water safe for drinking. Divide students into four groups. Direct one group to be the control group. Assign each of the remaining three groups one of the following filters to test: half cup of clean sand, a pinch of polyester fiberfill, or a coffee filter. Provide each group with the materials listed. Then guide the groups in completing the directions below.

Materials:
FOR EACH GROUP

16 oz. clear plastic cup
9 oz. paper cup
1 c. water mixed with ¹/₄ c. dirt

filter
permanent marker
sharp pencil

Directions:
1. Direct the groups to use the sharp end of the pencil to carefully make ten small holes in the bottom of the paper cup. Then have each group use the marker to label the plastic cup with either "control" or the name of the type of filter to be used.
2. Have the groups that are testing filters cover the bottom of the paper cup with the filter material. (The fiberfill and coffee filters should be placed in a single layer at the bottom of the cup.)
3. Instruct every group to hold its paper cup inside the plastic cup.
4. Have each group pour the muddy water into the paper cup and watch the water drain through the filter material. Then have the group observe the amount of material left in the filter and the color of the water in the plastic cup. (The control group should observe the amount of material remaining in the paper cup and the color of the water in the plastic cup.)
5. Position the cups side by side and allow each group to observe and compare them. Then have students compare the water of each filtered cup with the water in the control cup. *(The coffee filter is the best filter. The smaller spaces in the coffee filter make the water flow more slowly and trap more dirt.)*

Weather

Symbol Savvy

Here's a quick and simple idea that will give students practice making and interpreting weather symbols. Display a weather map from a local newspaper. Discuss with students how the different symbols represent weather patterns, such as the movement of warm and cold fronts, wind speed, cloud cover, rain, sun, and snow. Then provide each child with a map of the United States and an enlarged copy of the weather symbols shown. Direct the student to draw the symbols on the map to create a weather forecast. Then have each child use her map to write a detailed description of the predicted weather across the country. If desired, make a transparency of each map. Then set aside time for every student to act like a weather reporter as she explains the weather conditions on her map.

Weather Symbols

∞	Haze	⬥	Heavy rain
R	Thunderstorms	∿	Freezing rain
▽	Rain showers	△	Ice pellets, sleet
,,	Drizzle	✳ ✳	Light snow
∿	Freezing drizzle	✳✳	Moderate snow
▽	Snow flurries	✳✳	Heavy snow
≡	Fog	→	Drifting snow
R	Heavy thunderstorms with hail	▲▲▲	Cold front
)(	Funnel cloud(s)	▼▼▼	Stationary front
••	Light rain	⬛⬛	Warm front

©2000 The Education Center, Inc.

Hurricane and Tornado Facts

- several hundred miles in diameter
- winds over 300 miles per hour
- winds swirl around *eye*
- develops over warm ocean water
- sometimes called *cyclone* or *typhoon*
- usually occurs in the midwestern United States
- several hundred yards in diameter
- winds over 70 miles per hour
- can cause death and destruction
- usually lasts less than an hour
- sometimes called *twister* or *cyclone*
- produces huge waves, or storm surge
- grows weaker as it moves over land
- rotating funnel cloud

Tornado	Hurricane
winds over 300 miles per hour	several hundred miles in diameter
usually occurs in the midwestern United States	winds swirl around *eye*
several hundred yards in diameter	develops over warm ocean water
can cause death and destruction	sometimes called *cyclone* or *typhoon*
usually lasts less than an hour	winds over 70 miles per hour
sometimes called *twister* or *cyclone*	can cause death and destruction
rotating funnel cloud	produces huge waves, or storm surge
	grows weaker as it moves over land

"Storm-athon"

Your students will be blown away as they race to match the different characteristics of hurricanes and tornadoes in this fun game. Make a transparency of the storm facts shown. Have each child divide a sheet of paper into two columns. Direct the student to label one column "Hurricane" and the other "Tornado." Explain to students that you will show them several storm facts. Each fact describes either a hurricane or a tornado except one, which should to be written under both columns. Then display the transparency. When a student finishes writing the facts, collect his paper and record the time he finished. After all the papers are collected, call on student volunteers to help you write the correct storm name after each fact. If desired, give the student that recorded all of the facts correctly and in the least amount of time a small prize or treat.

Cool Clouds

No matter where you live, clouds are a visible sign of weather. So how do clouds form? This fiery demonstration will let students see a cloud form right before their eyes. Remind students that clouds occur when water vapor meets cooler air and condenses into water droplets or ice crystals. Then gather the materials listed and complete the following directions.

Materials:
large, clear glass jar with a straw-sized hole in the lid
straw
candle
matches
oven mitts

Directions:
1. Light the candle. Then, using the oven mitts, hold the jar mouth side down over the flame for at least 20 seconds.
2. Blow out the candle.
3. Place the lid on the jar and cover the hole with your finger. Allow the jar to cool for about a minute.
4. Insert the straw through the hole. Take a breath and exhale into the jar through the straw. Exhale into the straw three or four more times.
5. Position the jar on a flat surface where students can observe it. *(The air from inside the jar contains particles of soot from the candle. A cloud forms when the warm, moist air in the jar cools suddenly and condenses onto the soot particles. Condensation appears on the surface of the glass.)*

A Bit of a Breeze

Here's a hands-on review idea that will show students' understanding of how wind is created. Display the questions listed. Then pair students. Provide each pair with a balloon, a sheet of lined paper, and a pencil. Direct one student to blow up the balloon and pinch it closed with her fingers. As the pair works to answer the questions, have the partners record their answers on the paper.

Questions:
1. Touch the side of the inflated balloon. Is the high-pressure air inside or outside the balloon? *(inside the balloon)*
2. Place your hand near the opening of the balloon and then release the air inside. How was "wind" created? *(The high-pressure air inside the balloon rushed into the low-pressure area outside the balloon.)*
3. Why is it accurate to call the air rushing from the balloon wind? *(Wind is moving air. The air coming out of the balloon is moving.)*

Matter

Your Gift Matters!

Use students' love of birthday parties to help them remember the two basic characteristics of matter. First, remind students that matter is any object that has *mass* (weight) and *volume* (takes up space). Then have each child pretend she has been invited to a friend's birthday party. Have the student list five gifts she would like to give her friend. Next, have the student rank the gifts two ways: in order from the gift she thinks would have the greatest mass to the gift she thinks would have the least mass, and in order from the gift she thinks would have the greatest volume to the gift she thinks would have the least volume. Then provide each student with two index cards. Direct the child to decorate each card like a gift tag as shown, one card for her gift with the greatest mass, and the other card for her gift with the greatest volume. If desired, cover a bulletin board with colorful wrapping paper. Divide the board into two sections by placing a gift bow in each corner. Display the mass gift tags on one side of the board and the volume gift tags on the other. Title the board "Your Gift Matters!"

5 Gifts	Mass	Volume
1. CD	1. hairbrush	1. T-shirt
2. T-shirt	2. CD	2. necklace
3. hairbrush	3. T-shirt	3. CD
4. eye makeup	4. eye makeup	4. hairbrush
5. necklace	5. necklace	5. eye makeup

To My Friend
From Cayce
Most Mass
Happy Birthday!

To My Friend
From Cayce
Most Volume
Happy Birthday!

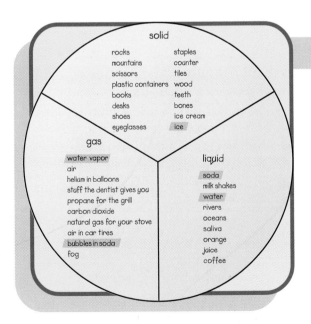

solid
rocks
mountains
scissors
plastic containers
books
desks
shoes
eyeglasses
staples
counter
tiles
wood
teeth
bones
ice cream
ice

gas
water vapor
air
helium in balloons
stuff the dentist gives you
propane for the grill
carbon dioxide
natural gas for your stove
air in car tires
bubbles in soda
fog

liquid
soda
milk shakes
water
rivers
oceans
saliva
orange
juice
coffee

Circular States

Here's a handy reference tool student pairs can make and use to remember the main states of matter. To begin, ask a student volunteer to describe water in each of its states of matter: liquid (water), solid (ice), and gas (water vapor). Then pair students and provide each pair with a large sheet of light-colored construction paper. Have the pair cut out a large circle from the paper. Then direct each pair to divide the circle in three sections as shown. Instruct the pair to label each section with one of the three main states of matter. Have partners list items found in each state of matter in each section of the circle. As an added challenge, direct students to highlight any item that is listed in more than one state. Display the circles around the classroom. Throughout the unit have students refer to their circles if they need to be reminded of the three main states of matter.

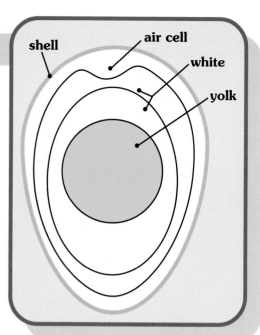

shell   air cell   white   yolk

"Egg-cellent Eggs-ample"

Need a quick way to model the three states of matter for your students? Look no further than the simple egg! To begin, make and display a transparency of the diagram shown. Point out to students that an egg contains all three states of matter. The shell represents the solid state. The white and the yolk represent the liquid state. The air cell between the white and the shell at the large end of the egg represents the gas state. Then pair students. Provide each pair with a sheet of white paper; a clean, raw, unbroken egg; a Styrofoam cup; a craft stick; a spoon (or another hard object to break the egg); and markers or crayons. (Before beginning the activity, remind students never to eat raw egg.)

Next, have each pair fold its paper in thirds. Direct the pair to observe the egg's shell and then draw and label the egg's solid state on the first section of its paper. Then have each pair carefully crack the egg at the middle with the spoon and pour the white and the yolk into the cup. Have the pair use the craft stick to break the yolk and stir the egg. Then the partners observe the contents of the cup and draw and label the egg's liquid state on the second section of the paper. Finally, instruct each pair to look into the large end of the shell for the air cell. Have the partners draw and label the egg's gas state on the third section of the paper. Three "egg-cellent" states of matter in one "incredible edible egg"!

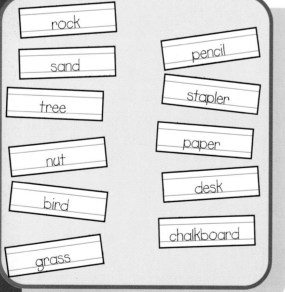

rock
sand
tree
nut
bird
grass
pencil
stapler
paper
desk
chalkboard

Property Race

Here's a fast-paced activity that will help your students better understand how matter can be sorted by its physical properties. To begin, give each student a half sheet of lined paper. Have him list as many items in a solid state as possible in one minute. Then have him cut his list apart so each item is on a separate strip of paper. Divide students into groups of four. Have each group combine its strips. On your signal, allow every group three minutes to divide the paper strips into two categories based on their common physical properties. Next, have the group remove the smaller of the two categories from the work area. Allow the group members three more minutes to divide the remaining strips into two different categories. Then ask a student volunteer from each group to share the two methods his group used to separate the strips by their common physical properties.

Changes That Matter

Here's an eye-popping demonstration that will allow your students to witness the two categories of properties of matter: physical and chemical. Begin by making and displaying a chart like the one shown. Then demonstrate a physical change and a chemical reaction by gathering the materials listed and following the directions below with the help of two student volunteers. Finally, ask students to name a physical change and a chemical reaction that occurred during the demonstration. *(Physical change: The balloon changed size and shape. Chemical change: The baking soda and the vinegar combined to form a new substance called carbon dioxide.)*

Is it a physical change or a chemical reaction?

- A physical change is a change in an object's appearance, but not in its chemical composition. *(A torn piece of paper is still a piece of paper.)*
- A chemical reaction usually occurs when two or more objects come into contact with each other and result in a new substance. *(When iron comes into contact with oxygen and water, rust is formed.)*

water and baking soda

vinegar and baking soda

Materials:
2 different-colored 12" balloons
$^1/_4$ c. water
$^1/_4$ c. vinegar
2 small funnels
2 tsp. baking soda

Directions:
1. Determine which balloon will be used with the water and which balloon will be used with the vinegar. Give each student volunteer a balloon.
2. Have each student place a funnel into the nozzle of his balloon.
3. Direct him to carefully pour one teaspoon of baking soda into the funnel. (If necessary, instruct the child to gently tap the funnel to help the baking soda move into the balloon.)
4. On your signal, have each student carefully pour the appropriate liquid into his funnel.
5. Direct the students to quickly remove the funnels and pinch off the nozzles of the balloons with their fingers.
6. Have the students gently shake the balloons to thoroughly mix the baking soda and the liquids.
7. Direct the student audience to observe the balloons. *(The vinegar balloon inflates while the water balloon remains the same shape.)*

Mixtures and Solutions

Snack Mixture

Mix in some fun with this introduction to mixtures. In advance, gather three large bowls, three different snack foods (such as pretzels, raisins, and chocolate chips), and a small cup for each student. Fill each bowl with a different snack. Place the bowls and cups on a table at the front of the room. Next, show students what is in each bowl. Explain that each snack represents a *compound*. Further explain that compounds can be combined to create mixtures and solutions. In a *mixture*, the compounds can be easily separated because they are not chemically combined. In a *solution,* one compound dissolves in another. In turn, have each student fill his cup with a small amount of each compound and return to his seat. Direct the student to place his hand over the top of the cup and shake the compounds until they are mixed. Ask students if they think they made a mixture or a solution and to explain why. *(They made a mixture. The compounds can be easily separated. Each compound is easily identified. The compounds are not chemically combined.)* Finally, let students enjoy the snack!

Evaporation Separation

Help students understand the characteristics of a solution with this simple activity. Ahead of time, make a solution of four cups Epsom salts and eight cups warm water. Explain to students that a *solution* is a type of mixture that is formed when one substance is dissolved in another. Give each student a small sheet of dark-colored construction paper, a paintbrush, and a small amount of the salt solution in a paper cup. Have each student observe the solution. Ask students whether they can easily distinguish the salt from the water. Then direct each student to brush the solution over her paper. Allow the papers to dry; then have each student observe the result. Ask students why the salt is easy to see now. *(The water evaporated, leaving behind the salt.)* Point out that compounds in a solution can be separated by evaporation.

Edible Mixtures and Solutions

Your students will be eager to learn about the difference between a mixture and a solution with this tasty activity. In advance, purchase a bag of chocolate chip cookies, powdered Kool-Aid mix, and sugar. Also gather a class supply of napkins, paper cups, and toothpicks.

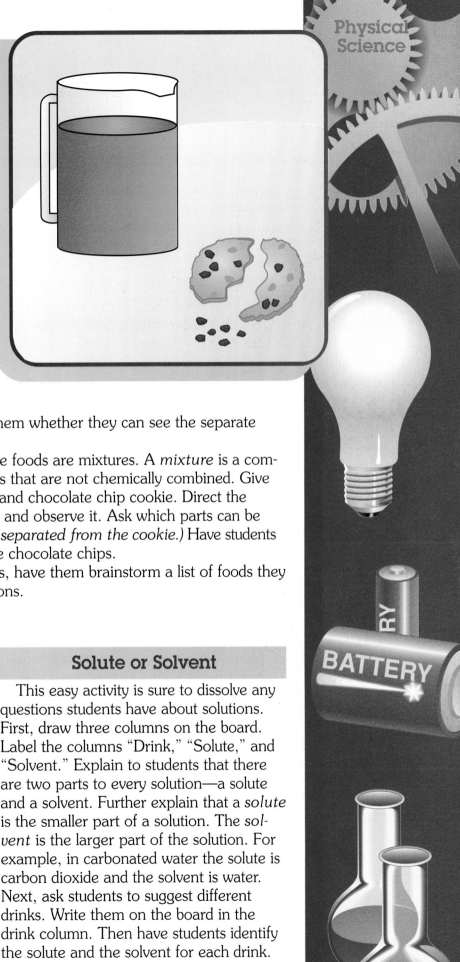

- Explain to students that some foods are solutions. A *solution* is a type of mixture formed when one substance dissolves into another. Demonstrate by making the Kool-Aid according to the packet directions. Then pour a small amount in a cup for each student. Have students observe the Kool-Aid. Ask them whether they can see the separate parts *(no)*.

- Next, explain to students that some foods are mixtures. A *mixture* is a combination of two or more substances that are not chemically combined. Give each student a napkin, toothpick, and chocolate chip cookie. Direct the student to break her cookie in half and observe it. Ask which parts can be easily separated. *(The chips can be separated from the cookie.)* Have students use their toothpicks to pick out the chocolate chips.

Finally, as students enjoy their snacks, have them brainstorm a list of foods they eat each day that are mixtures or solutions.

Drink	Solute	Solution
carbonated drink	carbon dioxide	water
lemonade	sugar, lemon juice	water
coffee	coffee grounds	water

Solute or Solvent

This easy activity is sure to dissolve any questions students have about solutions. First, draw three columns on the board. Label the columns "Drink," "Solute," and "Solvent." Explain to students that there are two parts to every solution—a solute and a solvent. Further explain that a *solute* is the smaller part of a solution. The *solvent* is the larger part of the solution. For example, in carbonated water the solute is carbon dioxide and the solvent is water. Next, ask students to suggest different drinks. Write them on the board in the drink column. Then have students identify the solute and the solvent for each drink.

Force, Energy, and Work

Machines Score a Touchdown!

Here's a fun, performance-based assessment task that measures students' understanding of the six simple machines: lever, wheel and axle, pulley, inclined plane, wedge, and screw. Challenge student pairs to draw a plan describing how to move a heavy box from one end of a football field to the other using all six simple machines. Ask each pair to present its plan to the class. If desired, display the drawings on a bulletin board titled "Machines Score a Touchdown!"

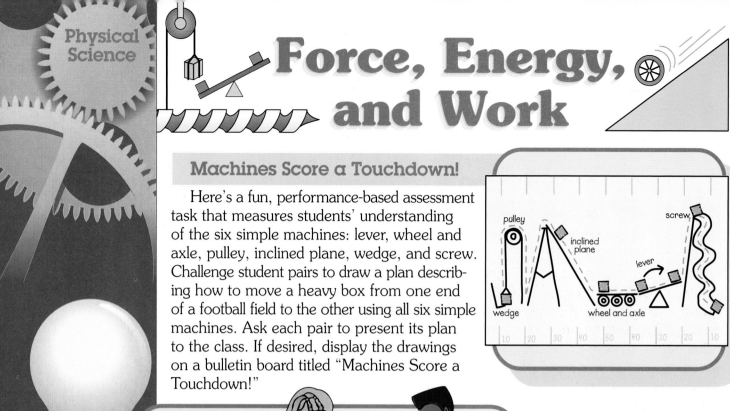

Fun With Force

Don't just give your students a definition of force—challenge them to discover it for themselves! Place the listed materials and a copy of the "Fun Force Tasks" shown at a center. Pair students. Have each pair visit the center in turn to complete the tasks. Then have the pair write its own definition of force based on the outcome of each task.

Figure 1

Figure 2

Figure 3

Materials:
2 sponge balls (palm-sized or smaller)
yardstick
stopwatch or watch with a second hand
tea towel or pillowcase

Fun Force Task 1: Position a tea towel or pillowcase flat on the floor. Place a ball in the center. Without lifting the towel completely off the floor, use vibrations to move the ball. (Figure 1)

Fun Force Task 2: Position a yardstick on the floor vertically as shown. Place a ball at one end. Rest your wrist on the floor and then flick the ball toward the opposite end of the stick. Time the ball's movement and note the distance it travels along the yardstick. Repeat the task twice, varying how you position your fingers when you flick the ball. (Figure 2)

Fun Force Task 3: Position the yardstick on the floor vertically as shown. Place the balls at opposite ends of the stick. Then, at the same time, have each partner flick a ball toward the other. Observe what occurs when the balls collide. Repeat the task, varying the amount of force used to flick each ball. (Figure 3)

Roll On!

Who wouldn't love to build and test his own roller coaster? Use this fast-paced activity to help students explore the concepts of *acceleration, deceleration, mass,* and *force.* To begin, explain to students that most moving items slow down and speed up, or decelerate and accelerate. The amount an object accelerates or decelerates is determined by its size or mass and by how much force is pushing or pulling it along. Divide students into four groups. Provide each group with a variety of empty tubes such as wrapping paper, paper towel, and toilet paper tubes. (Tubes approximately the same width work best.) Also give each group a stopwatch or watch with a second hand, a yardstick, tape, and a selection of small, round objects of various weights. (Each should be able to fit through the tube opening.) Direct the group to tape its tubes together to form a track. Then allow the group to position its track like a roller coaster around the room as desired. Have the group run each of the round objects down the track to test which travels faster and farther. Allow the groups to repeat the activity several times, modifying the position of the track each time. Finally, set aside time for the groups to share their results.

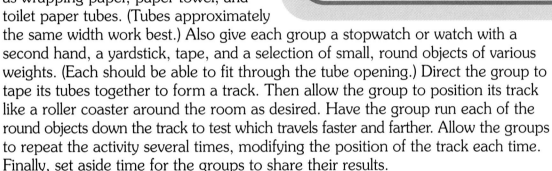

Boxed Energy

This large-group activity will allow your students to expend a little energy as they uncover the differences between potential and kinetic energy. Explain to students that *energy* is the ability to do work. There are two different types of energy: *kinetic energy,* the energy of motion, and *potential energy,* energy that is stored. Divide the students into four groups. Provide each group with a shoebox or paper bag containing the materials listed below. Set a timer or stopwatch for five minutes. Challenge the group to identify as many ways as possible each item in its box has potential and kinetic energy. Direct each group to list its responses on a sheet of notebook paper divided into two sections as shown. When time is up, ask a student volunteer from each group to share his group's items and results with the class.

Group 1:
rubber band
piece of charcoal
bottle of water

Group 2:
candle
battery
ruler

Group 3:
rubber ball
paper airplane
scissors

Group 4:
paper fan (made by accordion-
   folding a sheet of paper)
string
small piece of wood

Motion

Rating Motions

Get your motion unit really moving with this easy sorting game. Ahead of time program at least ten colorful index cards with the names of different items in motion, such as a speeding train, a beating heart, a movie, or a baseball struck by a bat. Then record a corresponding number of rates that would describe each motion on white index cards (for example, miles per hour, beats per minute, or feet per second). Put each set of cards in a resealable plastic bag; then write the directions below on a chartlet. After placing the bags and the directions at a center, pair students. Direct each pair to visit the center, in turn, and play the game.

beating heart	beats per minute
movie	feet per second
speeding train	miles per hour

Directions:
1. Remove the cards from the bag.
2. Shuffle each set of cards; then spread them out facedown on the playing surface.
3. To play, Player 1 turns over one colorful card and one white card. He determines whether the motion described on the colorful card matches the rate on the white card. If the cards match, he keeps them and takes another turn.
4. If the cards do not match, he turns the cards back over, and Player 2 takes a turn.
5. Play continues until all of the cards have been matched. The player with more cards is declared the winner.

All Aboard!

Let a little locomotion help your students learn about motion with this fun activity. Begin by explaining to students that motion is a change in an object's position over a certain amount of time. Some things appear to move fast and others seem to be slow, depending on the amount of time the movement takes. Write on the chalkboard the scenarios and questions listed below. Direct each student to read the scenarios and then answer the questions about distance and speed. Allow students to discuss their answers as a class.

Scenarios

Shoreliner Express traveled 80 miles. It took 40 minutes. *(2 miles per minute)*

Air Rail traveled 60 miles. It took 20 minutes. *(3 miles per minute)*

Viewliner travel 25 miles. It took 10 minutes. *(2.5 miles per minute)*

Questions

Which train traveled the farthest? *(Shoreliner Express)*

Which train would take the shortest amount of time if they each traveled 80 miles? *(Viewliner)*

Which train traveled at the fastest speed? Hint: Divide the distance by the time to find miles per minute. *(Air Rail)*

Move the Money

Give motion meaning with this "forceful" experiment. Review with students that force, or a push or pull, can stop movement, begin movement, or make something change direction. Then pair students. Provide each pair with four quarters, a ruler, paper, and a pencil. Direct one student to make a chart on the paper similar to the one shown. Have the other student position the ruler on a desk or tabletop. Have him begin at the two-inch mark and place three of the quarters beside, but not touching, the ruler as shown. Instruct the student to put the last quarter near the end of the ruler at zero inches. Have one student use his fingers to flick the first quarter toward the other coins at your signal. Have the pair record its observations on the chart. Direct the pair to repeat the experiment two times, applying increasing force to the first quarter with each turn. Finally, have each pair share its results with the class.

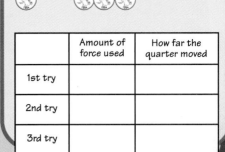

	Amount of force used	How far the quarter moved
1st try		
2nd try		
3rd try		

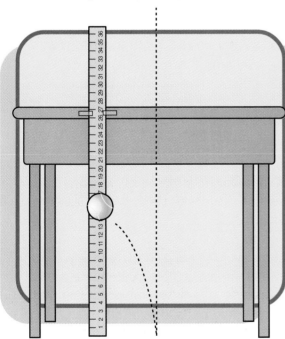

That's the Way the Ball Bounces

Here's an activity that is sure to show your students how environmental factors can affect movement. Ahead of time gather 15 new tennis balls. Place five of the balls in the freezer for at least 24 hours. Then, on the day of the activity, keep the balls cool until students use them. Ask students if they think a set of brand-new tennis balls will all bounce the same height. Divide the students into five groups. Give each group the materials listed below. Guide the groups through the directions shown. After completing the experiment, ask a student volunteer how she might alter her tennis game on a cold day. *(She would probably need to hit the ball harder to make it move the same distance it would travel on a warmer day.)*

Materials:

FOR EACH GROUP
cold tennis ball
2 tennis balls at room temperature
yardstick
tape
pencil
paper
access to a desk or table

Directions:
1. Tape the yardstick to the edge of the desk so the zero-inch end rests on the floor and the 36-inch end is at the top.
2. Choose one group member to drop each tennis ball.
3. Hold the first tennis ball at shoulder height in front of the yardstick and then drop it to the floor.
4. One group member records how high the ball bounces.
5. Drop the first ball two more times.
6. Mark a score for the first ball by averaging the heights that the ball bounced.
7. Repeat Steps 3 through 5 using the other two tennis balls.

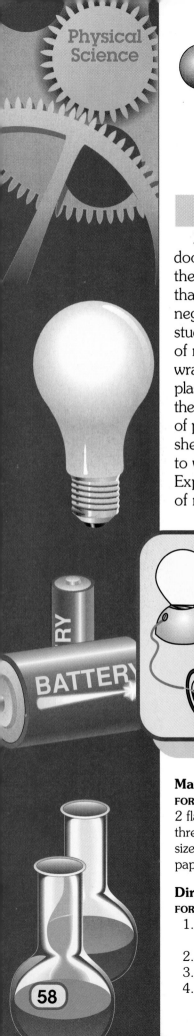

Electricity and Magnetism

"Ec-static" Electricity!

Zap! Ask students if they have ever touched a door handle and felt a tiny electric shock. If so, they've felt static electricity. Explain to students that *static electricity* is the buildup of positive or negative charges on an object. Next, give each student a handful of puffed rice cereal, two sheets of notebook paper, and a two-foot length of plastic wrap. Then instruct each student to ball up the plastic wrap and place the cereal on her desk. Direct the student to rub the plastic-wrap ball on one sheet of paper several times quickly and then hold the ball over the cereal. On the second sheet of paper, have the student record her observations and her conclusion as to why the cereal acted as it did. *(The cereal "sticks" to the plastic-wrap ball.)* Explain to your students that rubbing the ball on the paper gives the ball an excess of negatively charged electrons, which attracts the positively charged cereal.

Current Electricity

Help students discover how electrical currents flow in a series circuit with this activity. Divide your class into groups of four. Give each group the listed materials and guide them through the steps below. *(After completing the steps, students should observe that both lights go out when one bulb is unscrewed.)* Explain that electrical currents follow paths called circuits. Further explain that a *series circuit* uses a single path to connect everything. Therefore, if one lightbulb is unscrewed or burns out, the circuit is broken and all the bulbs will go out.

Materials:
FOR EACH GROUP
2 flashlight bulbs with holders
three 5" lengths of wire
size C battery
paper

Directions:
FOR EACH GROUP
1. Attach the wires to the battery and lightbulbs as shown. If the bulbs do not light, check the connections and try again.
2. While the bulbs are lit, unscrew one bulb.
3. Record your observations on a sheet of paper.
4. Record your conclusion about the bulb's reaction.

Fascinating Flashlight Facts!

Your students will be following a simple circuit in a flash with this flashlight activity. Divide students into groups of four. Give each group writing paper and a working plastic flashlight that uses size D batteries. Next, display a diagram of a flashlight on an overhead projector or a chalkboard as shown. Point out each of the labeled parts to students. Then instruct one student in each group to take apart the flashlight by removing the batteries and the bulb. Direct each student to write on a sheet of paper her hypothesis about how a flashlight works. After each student has shared her hypothesis, explain the facts below to students as you refer to the diagram.

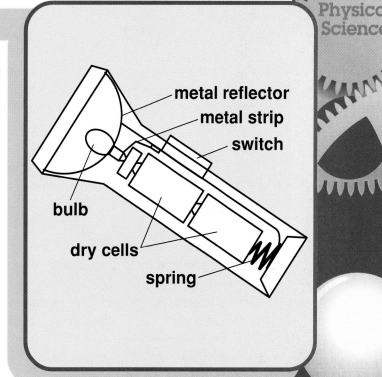

Flashlight Facts

1. The switch on the flashlight is connected to a metal strip that is part of a circuit.
2. One end of this metal strip touches the spring near the bottom of the flashlight, and the other end touches the bulb.
3. When you turn the switch to the on position, you open the circuit.
4. Charges flow from the battery to the metal spring, then to the metal strip that is part of the switch.
5. Charges move upward until they reach the metal of the bulb.
6. The charges enter the bulb, heat the thin wire inside, and move to the metal tip of the bulb.
7. There they enter the terminal at the top of the battery, causing the bulb to light.

May the Force Be With You

Magnets have force fields? Show your students a force field found in real life with this cleaner and easier version of the well-known iron-filings activity. Pair students. Then provide each pair with a plastic zippered bag, iron filings, and a magnet. Direct the partners to put the iron filings in the bag. Then have the pair set the bag on top of the magnet. (The iron filings will form a pattern to show the location of the north and south poles of the magnet. The largest clusters of filings will be around both poles.)

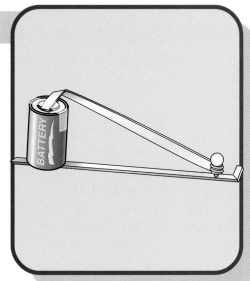

Lovely Light

Shed some light on simple circuits with this amazingly simple activity. Divide students into groups of five. Provide each group with the materials listed and a copy of the directions shown below. Remind students that the foil on top of the battery will become warm. To be safe, direct them to not leave the apparatus connected for more than one minute.

Materials:
FOR EACH GROUP
size C battery
2 strips of aluminum foil, each 15 cm long
clear tape
flashlight bulb

Directions:
1. Place the battery upright, with its flat end down, on one of the aluminum strips.
2. Roll one end of the other strip around the metal part of the lightbulb. Secure the strip with a piece of tape. (Check that the bulb's bump is sticking out.)
3. Tape the other end of the strip to the battery's bump. Touch the bulb to the strip that is under the battery. *(The bulb will light up.)*

A Whole Lot of Static

Do you have flyaway hair? Do you sometimes get shocked? Blame it on static electricity! Give students an opportunity to study static electricity with this intriguing small-group activity. Divide the students into groups of three. Give each group a gallon-sized resealable plastic bag, a handful of puffed rice cereal, and a small piece of wool fabric or fur. Direct one member from each group to place the cereal in the bag, gently inflate the bag with her breath, and then seal the bag. Have another group member create an electric charge by briskly rubbing the fabric against the bag for several minutes. Finally, have the last group member hold the charged bag in one hand while slowly bringing the fingertip of her other hand close to the bag. *(The bag is negatively charged after being rubbed with the fabric. The cereal is positively charged and sticks to the bag because opposites attract. When the student's positively charged finger comes close to the bag, the cereal jumps away because like charges repel one another.)*

Heat

Hot Heads

This easy idea will have your students using their heads to better understand how heat moves. Provide each student with a rubber band. Direct the student to place the band lengthwise across his forehead as shown. Ask a student volunteer whether the rubber band feels cool or warm *(cool)*. Then instruct each child to quickly, but carefully, stretch the band several times. Then have him place the rubber band back on his forehead. Ask another student volunteer whether the band feels cool or warm *(warm)*. Explain to students that every object contains moving molecules or atoms that give it *internal energy.* When the molecules move quickly, the object has higher internal energy, which makes it warmer. Similarly, if the molecules are moving slowly the object has low internal energy and feels cool.

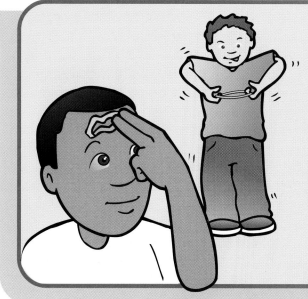

The Great Ice Race

Get things heated up with this cool race. First, remind students of the three ways heat can be transferred: *conduction, convection,* and *radiation.* Heat moving through a solid object, such as the bottom of a cooking pot, travels by conduction. Convection is the transfer of heat by a moving gas or liquid. Radiation is heat moving through space as energy waves. Divide students into groups of three. Provide each group with an ice cube, a plastic plate, and some paper towels. Next, assign every group either conduction, convection, or radiation. Explain to students that each group will race to try to make its ice cube melt the fastest. Allow groups to brainstorm different ways to melt their cubes for one minute (for example, by holding the ice cube in a group member's hand, blowing on the cube, or setting it on a sunny windowsill). Have students start the race on your mark. On the chalkboard, record the time it takes each group's cube to melt and the type of heat that was applied. Once a winning group is declared, allow students to discuss the different methods and results.

Heat Helps

Here's a hot tip: Heat makes water molecules move more quickly. Use this quick and easy demonstration to help students "see" water molecule movement. Gather ahead of time two clean, empty two-liter bottles, one packet of colored Jell-O, two funnels, and a teaspoon. On the day of the demonstration fill one of the bottles two-thirds full of cold water and the other bottle two-thirds full of hot water. Position the bottles where every student can see them. Allow the bottles to stand for 30 to 60 seconds. Then place a funnel in the neck of each bottle. Direct students' attention to the cold water. Carefully pour four to five teaspoons of Jell-O through the funnel and into the bottle. *(The Jell-O will sink to the bottom of the bottle.)* Next, pour the same number of tablespoons of Jell-O through the funnel and into the bottle of hot water. *(The Jell-O will move and spread through the hot water.)*

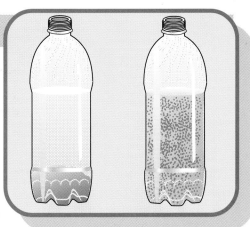

Hands Aren't Handy

Have you ever tried to tell the exact temperature of an object just by touching it? This simple small-group activity will show your students how their senses of touch can help determine whether an object is hot or cold, but not as reliably as a thermometer. Divide students into groups of three. Provide each group with the materials listed. Then guide students through the directions shown below.

Materials:
FOR EACH GROUP
3 Styrofoam bowls
permanent marker
masking tape
stopwatch or watch with a second hand
thermometer
access to very warm (but not steaming), cold, and
    tepid water

Directions:
1. Use the marker to write "hot," "cold," and "tepid" each on a piece of masking tape. Then attach one piece of tape to each bowl.
2. Carefully fill each bowl with the correct temperature of water. Use a thermometer to measure the temperature of the water in each bowl. Write the temperature on the corresponding piece of tape.
3. Place the bowls on a desk or tabletop.
4. Have one group member place each of her index fingers in the very warm and cold bowls for one minute.
5. Then have her place both fingers in the tepid water and describe the temperature. *(The tepid water will feel cool to the finger that was in the cold water and warm to the finger that was in the very warm water.)*
6. Allow every student to test the water temperatures by completing Steps 4 and 5 for each group member.

Light

Shed a Little Light

Pique students' interest in the subject of light with this exploratory activity. To begin, turn off several overhead lights and then turn on a flashlight. Point the flashlight at different items around the room. Ask students to consider why the light isn't visible behind you. *(A beam of light travels in a straight line.)* Then ask a student to turn the overhead lights back on. However, challenge the student to return to her seat before the lights shine. Have students consider why this is impossible. *(Light moves at a speed of up to 186,282 miles per second—much faster than a person can move!)* Pair students. Then provide each pair with the materials listed below and a copy of the directions shown to further explore the properties and behaviors of light.

Materials:
FOR EACH PAIR
flashlight
2 small pieces of transparency film
black and red permanent markers
paper
pencils

Directions:
1. Have each partner use a different-colored permanent marker to write his name, in large letters, on the transparency film.
2. With the classroom lights dimmed, have each partner take a turn shining the light on his name. Experiment projecting your names on and through different surfaces, changing the angle of the light and positioning the flashlight at various distances from the transparency film.
3. Record your observations.

2 + 3 = ? *(orange)*
1 + 2 = ? *(green)*
3 + 1 = ? *(violet)*

Color by the Numbers

Have you ever considered having a purple picnic? What about playing outside in the red light? Even though students can't see the different colors that make up white light, this demonstration will help them understand that light from the sun or a lamp appears colorless yet contains all the colors in the rainbow. To begin, show light separating through a prism. Explain to students that when a beam of light passes through a curved or angled surface, such as a raindrop or prism, its wavelengths are bent. The wavelengths spread out into the *visible spectrum* (rainbow) of red, orange, yellow, green, blue, indigo, and violet. Display on an overhead projector three circles cut from cellophane in the primary colors: red, blue, and yellow. Number each circle as shown. Program the questions above on a chalkboard. Ask student volunteers to come to the overhead and use the circles to solve each question.

Sound

Make That Sound Wave!

How are sounds different? Introduce students to the science behind sound as well as the term *frequency* with this ear-opening demonstration! First, make a simple instrument by placing several rubber bands of different widths around a small box. Position thicker rubber bands at one end and thinner rubber bands at the other end. Then instruct two student volunteers to hold a length of rope. Explain to students that the rope will represent different sound characteristics. Next, pluck the thin rubber bands on your instrument. Ask the students to demonstrate the sound waves for that high-pitched sound. Have one student move his end of the rope up and down quickly to create fast-moving waves. Pluck the thicker rubber bands on the instrument. Direct the student volunteer to make low-pitched waves in the rope by moving his end up and down slowly. Finally, explain to students that a sound's frequency is the number of waves that pass a certain point each second. High-pitched sounds have higher frequencies than low-pitched sounds.

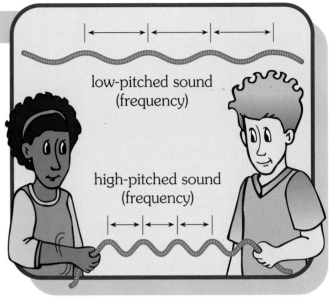

low-pitched sound (frequency)

high-pitched sound (frequency)

Good Vibrations

Help your students see that vibrations produce sound with this quick series of mini activities. Ahead of time, place the materials listed below at a center. Then pair students. Allow pairs to visit the center to complete the directions shown.

Materials:
2 metal dinner forks
clear container 1/3 full of water
Ping-Pong ball
9" length of string
tape
overhead projector

Directions:
1. With your teacher's help, turn on the overhead projector. Place the container of water on top of the projector.
2. Carefully strike one of the forks on the floor and then listen to the sound it makes.
3. Strike the fork again. Then lightly touch the fork to the surface of the water on the overhead projector. Observe how the water reacts. *(Vibration waves will be visible in the water.)*
4. Attach the string to the Ping-Pong ball with tape; then tape it to the "arm" of the overhead projector, suspending it above the water.
5. Strike the fork on the floor and then hold it close to the ball. Observe how the ball moves. *(It will shake or vibrate.)*
6. Finally, strike the fork again. Hold it close to the other fork. Use your fingers to pinch the first fork, stopping the vibration. Then listen to the other fork. *(The fork that wasn't struck will be vibrating.)*